T0149003

The Car Miscellany

THE
CAR
MISCELLANY

Simon Heptinstall

Published by AA Media Limited, whose registered office is
Grove House, Lutyens Close, Basingstoke, Hampshire, RG24 8AG;
registered number 06112600.

First published in 2019

10 9 8 7 6 5 4 3 2 1

A CIP catalogue record for this book is available from the
British Library.

ISBN: 978-0-7495-8184-8

Publisher: Phil Carroll (first car – Ford Focus 1.6 diesel)
Art Director: James Tims (first car – 1978 Mini Mk IV)
Editor: Clare Ashton (first car – Peugeot 105)
Design: Thomas Whitlock (first car – Vauxhall Nova)
Reprographics: Ian Little (first car – Ford Focus estate)

Printed and bound in the UK by Clays

A05571

Introduction

You might think you know a bit about cars – but did you know that the biggest tyre of all time is believed to be the Titan off-road mining model? It's 14ft tall and weighs more than six tons.

Or that the average modern car has about 30,000 parts, if you count all the tiniest screws and washers?

And that the smallest national road system in the world is in the Pacific nation of Tuvalu, which has just five miles of road? The US, by contrast, has more than four million miles of road.

Well, they do say that the devil is the detail. And they also say that little things make big things happen. So, if you want to really know about cars and motoring, perhaps eclectic little facts like those in this book might explain everything. Or maybe they are just interesting and don't actually explain anything at all.

In this book, like an aimless wandering road trip, I simply set out to record enjoyable, entertaining and educational facts, records and lists that I've accrued while researching books, magazines, interviews, websites and video footage. It's a traditional miscellany of motoring, an automobile almanac. I'm afraid that means this book is not authoritative, comprehensive or practical. It probably won't help you repair your car, choose your next vehicle or drive any better. *The Car Miscellany* is, however, full of devilish detail and little things that make some big things happen.

Enjoy.

Simon

Some facts about the author

He drives an ancient rusty
metallic maroon Volvo.

**He has compiled a list of the
worst-ever dashboards.**

His greatest triumphs have been
producing a collection of the world's greatest
cars as cardboard cut-out models and driving a
supercar around the Millbrook test track with
a plastic cone stuck underneath the car.

The 10 ugliest cars of all time

(the author's personal choice)

Fiat Multipla

AMC Pacer

BMW 1 Series Hatchback

Aston Martin Lagonda

1980 Cadillac Seville

Nissan S-Cargo

SsangYong Rodius

Pontiac Aztek

Austin Allegro Vanden Plas

Audi Q7

The word 'car' derives from the
Latin word 'carrus' used
by Romans to describe a
horse-drawn wheeled cart.

Fuel facts

* Half of all new cars sold in Norway are either fully electric or hybrid-powered.

* Around 92% of all cars sold in Brazil can run on ethanol fuel produced from sugar cane.

* From 2003 to 2014 everyone in Turkmenistan was entitled to 120 litres (31 gallons) of free petrol every month.

* In 1900, less than a quarter of American cars were powered by petrol. More than a third were powered by electricity and 40% were powered by steam.

* In 2009, a British team built a car with a 12-boiler engine running on steam power. It was the equivalent of boiling 1,500 kettles at once and powered the car across the Mojave Desert in California at 148mph.

* In 1973, the average American car's fuel economy was 16mpg.

A Chinese truck driver was arrested for kidnapping two toll-station operators to save paying the equivalent of 70p.

The Koenigsegg CCXR Trevita (2007) had a unique body made using a technique of coating the carbon fibres with diamonds to create a shimmering finish. The car retailed at more than £3 million.

Cars with place names

Morris – Oxford

Austin – Cambridge

Cadillac – Seville

Seat – Cordoba

Ford – Cortina

Triumph – Dolomite

Ferrari – Modena

Hyundai – Santa Fe

Seat – Marbella

Toyota Landcruiser – Colorado

Seat – Ibiza

Alfa Romeo – Montreal

Austin – Somerset

Lancia – Monte Carlo

Seat – Toledo

Lada – Samara

Austin – Montego

Ferrari – California

Vauxhall – Monterey

Subaru – Tribeca

Chevrolet – Tahoe

Austin – Westminster

Ford – Granada

Hyundai – Tucson

Panther – Lima

Seat – Alhambra

Ford – Anglia

Porsche – Cayman

Rolls Royce – Camargue

Kia – Rio

Seat – Leon

Volvo – Amazon

The year of the bull

Italian rural tractor producer Ferruccio Lamborghini was always rather fond of bulls. His star sign was Taurus and he was fascinated by bullfighting. He visited a fighting-bull ranch owned by Don Eduardo Miura, near Seville in Spain, that had been breeding famously fierce fighting bulls since 1842. The next year, in 1963, Lamborghini launched a car-making business and chose one of Miura's fighting bulls as his car badge. The company went on to become one of the biggest names in supercars, naming many of its models after famous bulls. Lamborghini even named the Miura after Don Eduardo.

Biggest tyre companies in the world (By sales 2017)

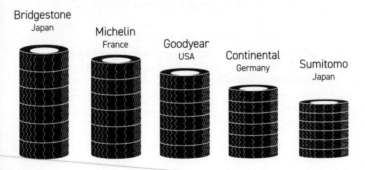

Bridgestone
Japan

Michelin
France

Goodyear
USA

Continental
Germany

Sumitomo
Japan

Three points of law

In **Alaska**, it is illegal to drive with a dog tied to the roof of your vehicle.

In **Sweden**, it's a legal requirement to drive with your lights on all day long.

In **Spain**, if you wear glasses you are legally obliged to carry a spare set in your car.

Six cars owned
by dictators

Mercedes-Benz G4 staff car – Adolf Hitler (d. 1945)
Hitler had a six-wheel-drive Mercedes reinforced with
bulletproof glass that did 7.8mpg.

ZIS-115 – Joseph Stalin (d. 1953)
The ZIS-115 model was designed and built especially
for Stalin. It was based on stolen designs for a US Packard but
weighed more than eight tons and had glass so thick the
windows were powered by hydraulic motors.

Mercedes-Benz Limousine – Pol Pot (d. 1998)
The leader of the Khmer Rouge was a staunch fan of
Mercedes-Benz and owned a fleet, all in black.

Range Rover – Idi Amin (d. 2003)
Amin was worried about assassination so used a heavily
fortified Range Rover with a forest of antennas and spotlights.
Inside were grenades, pistols and knives. After fleeing Uganda
for sanctuary in Saudi Arabia, Amin retired with a white
Chevrolet Caprice and a powder-blue Cadillac.

Mercedes-Benz ML – Muammar Gaddafi (d. 2011)
Gaddafi's military-spec Mercedes-Benz ML cost £3.5m and
had a protective cage and radio-wave scrambler technology
to defy drones and guided missiles.

Nissan Patrol 4x4 – Kim Jong-Il (d. 2011)
Kim Jong-Il had a personal vehicle collection valued at
$20m, including several Nissan Patrol 4x4s equipped for
catering and dining. His son, Jong-un, has expanded that to
include a special Mercedes long-wheelbase limousine, several
Lamborghinis, and a mobile toilet that follows him everywhere.

The first car race in America was held during such a severe snowstorm that two contestants lost consciousness due to exposure. The 1895 race from Chicago to Evanston was won by inventor James Frank Duryea, who completed the 54-mile route in 10 hours 23 minutes at an average speed of 5.25mph.

Top 10 hot hatchbacks of all time*

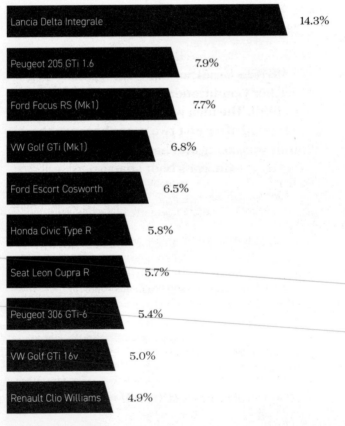

Lancia Delta Integrale	14.3%
Peugeot 205 GTi 1.6	7.9%
Ford Focus RS (Mk1)	7.7%
VW Golf GTi (Mk1)	6.8%
Ford Escort Cosworth	6.5%
Honda Civic Type R	5.8%
Seat Leon Cupra R	5.7%
Peugeot 306 GTi-6	5.4%
VW Golf GTi 16v	5.0%
Renault Clio Williams	4.9%

*as voted for by *Autocar* readers

Fitting extravagant extras is not a modern phenomenon. In the 1920s, car manufacturers tried to seduce buyers with bizarre bolt-on extras like bells, klaxons and compasses. Some Rolls Royces even had dashboard gun-mounts for tiger shooting in India.

Through the 50s and 60s buyers were offered eye-catching oddities like atomic bomb denotation warning lights or built-in barometers. And in the 1970s, General Motors offered optional tents built into the tailgate of some cars to allow owners to sleep in the boot.

Packard became the first manufacturer to offer air conditioning, with a pioneering 'Weather Conditioner' unit making its debut in 1939. The idea was a disaster and was scrapped after just two years because the unit was so big and heavy it took up half the car's boot space.

Skoda's most luxurious trim level is named Laurin & Klement. This is the name of the original company founded in 1895 in what was then the Austro-Hungarian Empire, making Skoda one of the world's oldest companies still producing cars. The company founders were Vaclav Klement and Vaclav Laurin.

The Sheikh Khalifa motorway in Abu Dhabi has a 100mph speed limit.

Luxury optional extras

Seats that adjust side-to-side	Mercedes
'Airscarf' neck heating system	Mercedes
See-through bonnet	Lamborghini
Choose exact number of coats of paint	Ferrari
Double-glazed windows	Audi
Porcelain caviar tray	Bugatti
Leather door handles similar to Hermès luggage	Bugatti
Granite trim	Maybach
Golden keys	Maybach
On-board perfume atomiser	Maybach
Leather flooring	Rolls Royce
Bespoke pen set in glove box	Rolls Royce
Umbrella in door pocket	Rolls Royce
Blue illuminated bonnet statuette	Rolls Royce
Transponder watch/remote car control	Aston Martin
Wood-veneer drinks cabinet	Overfinch
Boot-mounted shotgun case	Overfinch

Volkswagen sells more sausages than cars. The German manufacturer sells more than 7 million 'currywurst' VW-branded sausages a year.

Top 10 cheapest cars to insure in the UK in 2018

1. Skoda Citigo/Volkswagen up! 1.0
2. Ford Ka+ 1.2 Studio
3. Nissan Micra 1.0
4. Volkswagen Polo 1.0
5. Hyundai i10 1.0
6. Vauxhall Corsa 1.4 Sting
7. Ford Fiesta 1.1 Style
8. Dacia Logan 1.0 Access
9. Renault Twingo 1.0 Expression
10. Toyota Yaris 1.0 Active

*List compiled by *AutoExpress* magazine

The average distance cycled per person in Britain every year is 39 miles. Comparable methods of movement include walking, with an average of 189 miles per person, bus 342 miles and train 368 miles, while average car travel is 5,354 miles per person.

Bertha Benz, the wife of colourful inventor Karl, was the first person to take a proper journey in an automobile. In 1888, she took her husband's prototype vehicle without him knowing and drove her two teenage sons along wagon tracks for 66 miles from Mannheim to Pforzheim in Germany. In 2008, the journey was celebrated with the establishment of the Bertha Benz Memorial Route following her journey, which includes signs showing where she stopped to buy fuel from a chemist and cleaned a blocked fuel pipe with her hat pin.

RAF Hethel in Norfolk was used by US Air Force bombers during World War II. After the war, it was used to house Polish refugees. In 1966, it became the headquarters of Lotus cars, which still uses the runway for testing.

---

15 famous people killed in motoring accidents

Name	Occupation	Vehicle
Mark Bolan	pop star	Mini
Albert Camus	writer	Facel Vega
Eddie Cochran	pop star	Ford Consul
Laurie Cunningham	footballer	Renault 5 GTi
James Dean	actor	Porsche 550
Diana, Princess of Wales	royal	Mercedes S280
Alexander Dubcek	Czech politician	BMW 535
Isadora Duncan	dancer	Amilcar
Grace Kelly	actor/royal	Rover P6
T E Lawrence	of Arabia	Brough Superior
Jayne Mansfield	actor	Buick Electra
General George Patton	military leader	Cadillac 75
Jackson Pollock	artist	Oldsmobile 88
Cozy Powell	drummer	Saab 9000
Paul Walker	actor	Porsche Carrera

Six longest car races in the world

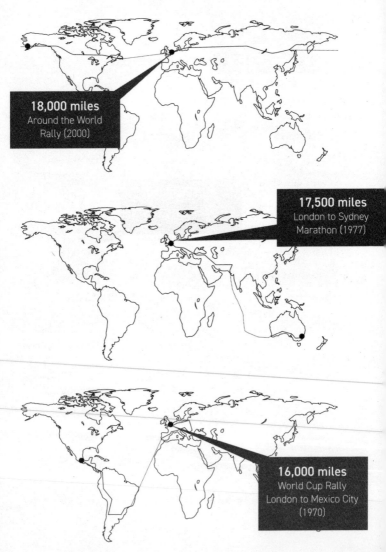

18,000 miles
Around the World
Rally (2000)

17,500 miles
London to Sydney
Marathon (1977)

16,000 miles
World Cup Rally
London to Mexico City
(1970)

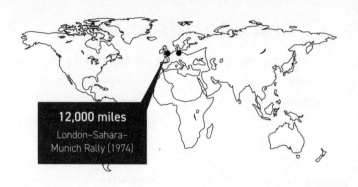

12,000 miles
London–Sahara–
Munich Rally (1974)

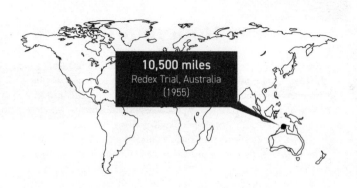

10,500 miles
Redex Trial, Australia
(1955)

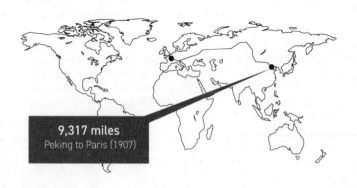

9,317 miles
Peking to Paris (1907)

Road-going production cars without doors

Bond Minicar 1949	**Caterham 7** 1973
Allard Clipper 1953	**Mitsuoka MC-1** 1998
Brütsch Mopetta 1956	**Ariel Atom** 2000
Lotus 7 1957	**Westfield Megabusa** 2000
Goggomobil Dart 1959	**Smart Crossblade** 2002
Peel Trident 1964	**Renault Twizy** 2012
Ford Bronco U13 1966	**Morgan 3 Wheeler** 2018

The Popemobile

The Popemobile is a one-off Mercedes built for the head of the Roman Catholic church to be used while touring. Despite its normal sedate progress of around 6mph, the £200,000 vehicle is powered by a 5.5-litre V8 engine capable of 155mph, and can potentially accelerate from 0–60mph in six seconds. In the 1970s, the Pope was simply carried on a chair on papal attendants' shoulders, but the heavily customised Mercedes M-Class SUV was ordered after a 1981 assassination attempt. It features armour plating, including a half-inch-thick steel bomb guard underneath, and a kevlar cabin. It has three-inch-thick bulletproof glass, run-flat tyres (capable of 70mph) and a separate air supply in case of gas or chemical attack.

The Pope enters through a rear tailgate door and sits in a normal rear passenger position for day-to-day transportation. He can then be raised by hydraulic motors into the glass turret to be seen by crowds. The interior is trimmed in white leather and contains built-in religious icons. The personalised number plate reads 'SCV 1' – signifying the Pope's position in the Vatican City State. In Mexico and the Philippines, the Popemobile has been on display so devout local Catholics could make pilgrimages to see the car and feel spiritually close to the Holy Father.

A few European motoring laws

(!) In France, some streets have *stationnement alterne semi-mensuel* or alternate parking systems. It means that from 1st to 15th of the month you can park on one side of the road, and from 16th to the end on the other.

(!) In Russia, traffic lights flicker green before changing to yellow, then red.

(!) In Germany, you can be fined for running out of fuel on the autobahn.

(!) In Luxembourg, you must flash your headlamps when overtaking at night.

(!) In Spain, non-resident motorists can get an on-the-spot fine of up to €600 for driving violations, with 20% off for immediate settlement. The police can even escort you to the nearest cash machine in order to pay.

(!) In France, anyone caught travelling at more than 25kph above the speed limit can have their licence confiscated on the spot.

(!) In Belgium, if you are found with between 0.05% and 0.08% alcohol in your blood you have to surrender your licence for three hours.

(!) In Spain, truck drivers signal right when it's safe to overtake them, left when it's not.

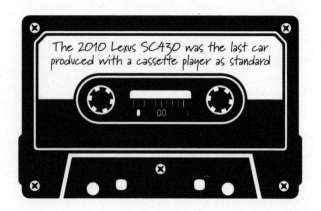

The 2010 Lexus SC430 was the last car produced with a cassette player as standard

Top 10 most reliable cars in the UK

1. Toyota IQ
2. Mitsubishi Lancer
3. Vauxhall Agila
4. Hyundai Getz
5. Honda Jazz
6. Nissan Almera Tino
7. Hyundai i10
8. Mercedes CLC
9. Mazda MX-5
10. Citroën C1

And the bottom 10

1. Maserati Granturismo
2. BMW M5
3. BMW M6
4. Nissan GT-R
5. Mercedes CL
6. Aston Martin DB9
7. Mercedes GL
8. Bentley Continental GT
9. Mercedes R-Class
10. Citroën C6

as listed on reliabilityindex.com

The Ital Job

The Morris Ital was a popular family saloon built by British Leyland from 1980 to 1984 (and until 1998 in China). It was named after the fashionable Ital design studio run by Giorgetto Giugiaro, although the car was actually designed by Londoner Harry Mann. The rear-wheel-drive car came as a saloon, estate, pickup or van and offered petrol engines ranging from 1275cc up to two litres. More than 175,000 were built before it was axed. It was the last car to be badged as a Morris. The car had a bad reputation for rust, however, and in 2008 was voted second in a poll of 'the worst British car ever'. This has helped make it one of the fastest disappearing mainstream cars of modern times. At the time of writing only 37 Itals are still registered on the UK's roads.

Great film car chases

The Blues Brothers (1980)
1974 Dodge Monaco sedan | New York | 3:50

Bourne Identity (2002)
Mini Cooper | Paris | 4:02

Bullitt (1968)
1968 Ford Mustang 390 GT 2+2 Fastback | San Francisco | 10:07

The French Connection (1971)
Lincoln Continental Mark III | New York | 5:32

The Italian Job (1968)
Mini Coopers | Rome | 10:23

Mad Max 2 (1981)
Ford Falcon XB GT Coupé | Western Australia | 1:57

Ronin (1998)
Peugeot 406 & BMW 535i | Paris | 7:03

Taken 2 (2012)
Mercedes W124 Taxi | Paris | 2:36

To Live and Die in L.A. (1985)
Lincoln Continental | Los Angeles | 3:12

Vanishing Point (1997)
1970 Dodge Challenger | Nevada | 4:53

Hot hatching

The first hot hatch (a hatchback with enhanced performance) is generally considered to be the Autobianchi A112 Abarth, which was introduced by Fiat in 1971 after the engineers in its motorsport division were able to increase the power of the small 982cc engine from 58hp to 70hp. The tiny three-door hatchback featured a scorpion badge, was nicknamed 'the pocket Ferrari' and was the first car for many racing drivers of the era.

Top four global car-making groups by million vehicles built per year

1 – **Volkswagen Group** – 10.74

2 – **Renault / Nissan / Mitsubishi** – 10.61

3 – **Toyota** – 10.47

4 – **General Motors** – 9.6

---

10 famous fictional cars

Lightning McQueen from *Cars*

Chitty Chitty Bang Bang

Doc Brown's Delorean from *Back to the Future*

James Bond's Aston Martin DB5

Herbie the Love Bug

Batman's Batmobile

The Mystery Machine from the *Scooby Doo* cartoons

KITT from the *Knight Rider* TV show

The flying Ford Anglia from *Harry Potter*

The Flintmobile from *The Flintstones* cartoon

One of the main characters in the 2006 animated film *Cars* is Doc Hudson, the local judge in the desert town Radiator Springs. Doc Hudson is voiced by actor and racing driver Paul Newman. The unassuming old car turns out to be an accomplished race winner from the past. The character is actually based on a true story. The Hudson Hornet was an all-conquering NASCAR competitor in the 1950s. Despite Hudson's success on the track, the small independent manufacturer was taken over and disappeared in 1957.

Cars once owned by motoring celebrity Jeremy Clarkson

Volvo XC90, Range Rover TDV8 Vogue SE, Lotus Elise 111S, Mercedes 600 Grosser, Mercedes SLK55 AMG, Mercedes CLK63 Black, Mercedes SLS AMG Roadster, BMW M3 CSL, Honda CR-X, Ferrari F355, Ford GT, Aston Martin Virage, Alfa Romeo Alfetta GTV6, Ford Focus, Lamborghini Gallardo, VW Golf GTI, VW Scirocco Mk 1, VW Scirocco Mk 2, Land Rover Defender, Ford Escort RS Cosworth, McLaren 675LT, Toyota Land Cruiser.

After World War II, the British economy was desperate for an injection of cash, so the government ordered car makers to concentrate on exports. In 1950, more than two-thirds of cars made in Britain were sold to America.

Der Nurburgring

The 13-mile Nurburgring public circuit through the woods of western Germany is often used to test cars. Drivers and manufacturers vie to complete the demanding circuit in the fastest possible time.

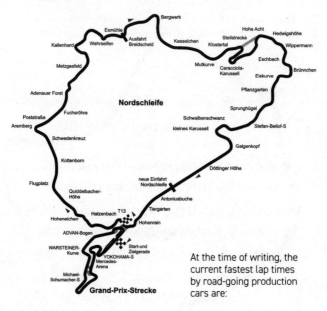

At the time of writing, the current fastest lap times by road-going production cars are:

6m 44s
Lamborghini Aventador LP 770-4 Superveloce (2018)

6m 47s
Porsche 911 GT2 RS (2017)

6m 48s
Radical SR8 LM (2009)

6m 52s
Lamborghini Huracán LP 640-4 Performante (2016)

6m 55s
Radical SR8 (2005)

6m 56s
Porsche 911 GT3 RS (2018)

6m 57s
Porsche 918 Spyder (2013)

6m 59s
Lamborghini Aventador LP 750-4 Superveloce (2015)

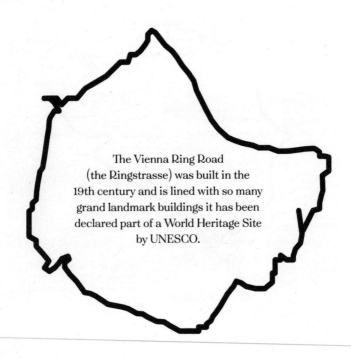

The Vienna Ring Road
(the Ringstrasse) was built in the
19th century and is lined with so many
grand landmark buildings it has been
declared part of a World Heritage Site
by UNESCO.

Sleepy signs

Across Britain's motorway network there are 57 signs saying "Tiredness can kill, take a break". They are usually placed two miles before a service area and are designed to remind drivers to take a break without leading to large numbers stopping at inappropriate places. According to experts at motorwayservicesonline.co.uk there is a 'Tiredness' sign on the M5 nowhere near a service station, but it could be there simply because that stretch of road is particularly dull.

The 1962 Oldsmobile Jetfire F-85, a hardtop sporty version of the Cutlass, was the first production car fitted with a turbo. Nicknamed 'Turbo Rocket', the F-85 had bucket seats and a turbo gauge on the console, but no rev counter, and used the standard car's sedate automatic gearbox and soft suspension. *Car and Driver* tested the Jetfire and recorded a 110mph top speed and 0–60mph time of 9.2 seconds. The high price and unreliable turbo limited its success and it was withdrawn after selling less than 4,000 units.

Hot car

The highest price paid for a Hot Wheels toy car was $70,000 in 2000 for a pre-production version of a Volkswagen Beach Bomb. This was a VW microbus with a pair of surfboards poking out of the rear window. This design failed initial testing, proving to be top-heavy, and a widened version with the surfboards mounted in side slots was released in 1969. The rear loader version is a very sought-after vehicle among Hot Wheels collectors. There are only about 50 believed to be in existence.

"Straight roads are for fast cars,
turns are for fast drivers."

Colin McRae

Entry fees

Think tickets for F1 Grand Prix races are expensive? Spare a thought for the race teams. All teams have to pay an entry fee to compete. This involves a basic fee plus extra based on where they finished in the previous season. In 2019, the fees were:

Mercedes
$4.8m (£3.6m)

Ferrari
$3.6m (£2.7m)

Red Bull
$2.8m (£2.1m)

Renault
$1.2m (£0.9m)

Haas
$1.1m (£0.8m)

McLaren
$0.9m (£0.7m)

Racing Point
$0.8m (£0.6m)

Sauber
$0.8m (£0.6m)

Toro Rosso
$0.7m (£0.5m)

Williams
$0.6m (£0.4m)

Seven strange smells that show something is wrong with your car

Burning – could be leaking oil dripping onto a hot exhaust

Rotten eggs – often caused by a defective catalytic converter

Sickly sweet – likely to be a leakage of coolant or antifreeze

Old musty smell – can be caused by mould in the air-con

Burning carpet – might be a brake problem

Burnt rubber – could be a slipping belt in the engine bay

Petrol – either you've just filled up and spilt a bit or you may have a dangerous fuel leak

A coupe de ville was originally a horse-drawn carriage with the driver's position open-topped and the passengers' compartment covered. This stylish urban form of transport derived its name from the French 'ville' for 'town'. This in turn later gave rise to the name of the Lincoln Town Car built by Ford in America from 1981 to 2011, although in this case the Lincoln's driver wasn't left exposed to the elements.

A survey of 2,000 UK drivers discovered some of the most annoying habits exhibited by passengers. These included:

Frequent displays of exaggerated emotion

Gasping loudly when the driver brakes

Complaining about speed

Stamping on an imaginary brake pedal

Flinching when they appear to drive 'too close' to the car in front

Pointing out the correct turn-off

Being involved in road rage on the driver's behalf

Holding hands over their face

Giving directions when they are not needed

The UK's narrowest new cars

1. Renault Twizy

1396mm

2. Kia Picanto

1595mm

3. Vauxhall Viva

1595mm

4. Suzuki Celerio

1600mm

5. Citroën C1/Peugeot 108/Toyota Aygo

1615mm

Ford's soya car

Henry Ford built a car made from soya bean fibres. The Soybean Car was unveiled by Ford on 13 August 1941, at Dearborn, Michigan. The tubular steel frame had 14 plastic panels attached. The car weighed just 2,000lbs, 1,000lbs lighter than an equivalent car with steel panels. It is believed that the panels were made from soyabean fibre and resin. Henry Ford was looking for a project to combine the fruits of industry with agriculture and there was a shortage of metal at the time. The imminent outbreak of World War II suspended all car production, and although a second unit was being built when war broke out, the project was abandoned and the prototypes destroyed.

Celebrity car endorsements

Jude Law – **Lexus RX**

Jennifer Lopez – **Fiat 500**

Chuck Norris – **Fiat vans**

Andy Murray – **Jaguar XF Sportbrake**

Wayne Rooney – **Ford Ka**

Justin Timberlake – **Audi A1**

Victoria Beckham – **Range Rover Evoque**

Kylie Minogue – **Lexus CT200h**

Thierry Henry – **Renault Clio**

Delia Smith – **Proton Gen2**

Jose Mourinho – **Jaguar F-Type Coupé**

The Royal Automobile Club, the RAC, was established by engineer Fred Simms in 1897.
The Automobile Association, the AA, was launched by a group of motoring enthusiasts in 1905.

Crime fighters driving classic cars

Morse	Jaguar Mark II
Starsky and Hutch	1975 Ford Gran Torino
Bergerac	1949 Triumph Roadster
The Saint	1962 Volvo P1800
Saga Noren	1977 US-spec Porsche 911S
Magnum PI	Ferrari 308 GTS
Frank Bullitt	Ford Mustang 390 GT
Columbo	1959 Peugeot 403 Cabriolet
The Professionals	Mark III Capri 3.0S
The Sweeney	Granada S and Granada Ghia
Michael Knight	Pontiac Firebird Trans Am (KITT)
Gene Hunt	Ford Cortina and Audi Quattro
George Gently	Rover P5 Mark II/Mark III
Charlie's Angels:	
Jill & Kris	Ford Cobra II
Kelly	Ford Mustang
Sabrina, Tiffany & Julie	Ford Pinto
Bosley	Ford Thunderbird
Emma Peel	1962 Lotus Elan
Inspector Lewis	Vauxhall Insignia
Sonny Crockett	1972 Ferrari Daytona Spyder 365 GTS
Kurt Wallander	Volvo XC70
Jim Rockford	Pontiac Firebird Esprit

The average car is parked
for 95% of its lifetime.

Notable advertising slogans

The power of dreams	Honda
Driven by passion	Fiat
Volvo. For life.	Volvo
The Ultimate Driving Machine	BMW
Vorsprung durch technik	Audi
Surprisingly ordinary prices	VW
The drive of your life	Peugeot
The car in front is a Toyota	Toyota
Go beyond	Land Rover
A class of its own	Rover
You can with a Nissan	Nissan
The power to surprise	Kia
It's a Skoda. Honest.	Skoda
Grab life by the horns	Dodge
Isn't it time for a real car?	Buick
Find your own road	Saab
Like nothing else	Hummer
Auto emocion	Seat
Zoom zoom	Mazda
Think small	VW
Grace, space, pace	Jaguar
Va va voom	Renault
Your mother wouldn't like it	MG

Legally the hard shoulder of a motorway has a speed limit of 70mph. This is to allow a car or motorbike to speed up to rejoin the flow of traffic.

Still going...

The longest ever journey by car is still being made in a Toyota Land Cruiser. According to the *Guinness Book of Records*, Emil and Liliana Schmid have now covered 474,000 miles on one single continuous journey since 1984, crossing 348 international borders and using 31,000 gallons of fuel in the process. "We wanted to swap routine and security for adventure and freedom," they said when they started. So the Swiss couple bought a Toyota Landcruiser FJ60 and set out on 16 October 1984 to explore the world. They're still going and recently said "the spirit of adventure is still unbroken".

Four facts about the Ford Escort

1. The original Mark I Ford Escort was one of the first global cars. It was built in the UK, Australia, New Zealand, Belgium, Ireland, Taiwan and Israel.

2. Princess Diana owned a black Mark I Escort RS Turbo – the only black version that Ford built, all others being white.

3. The Escort was launched in 1967 as a rear-wheel-drive car. The third generation, in 1980, switched to front-wheel drive.

4. Hannu Mikkola's Escort won the World Cup Rally from London to Mexico in 1970; other Escorts came 3rd, 5th, 6th and 8th. The success prompted Ford to launch the special Escort Mexico model.

10 current cars destined to become classics

Suzuki Swift (2005–2011)

Nissan Skyline GT-R (1993–1998)

Mazda RX-7 (1992–2002)

BMW 1 Series M Coupé (2011)

Renault Clio V6 (2001–2005)

Ford Fiesta ST (2013–2017)

Ferrari 458 (2009–2015)

Alfa Romeo Giulia Quadrifoglio (2016–present)

Honda S2000 (1999–2009)

Lotus Exige S2 (2004–2006)

according to carkeys.co.uk

Car names inspired by music

Honda Prelude, Hyundai Sonata, Kia Forte, Ford Tempo,
Honda Concerto, Nissan Note, Kia Cadenza, Honda Beat,
Buick Encore, Honda Ballade, Toyota Duet, Tata Aria,
Austin Allegro, Honda Jazz, Honda Quintet

The top-selling Nissan of all time is not the
globally successful Sunny, Micra or Bluebird.
It's the Qashqai crossover (2006–present)
with 3.7 million sales to date.

Drag stars

No other ground vehicle in the world can out-accelerate today's top-fuel dragsters. They sprint from 0–60mph in an incredible 0.3 seconds. In comparison, the latest and fastest-ever Porsche 911 Turbo takes 2.9 seconds to reach 60mph (96kph) – by which time the dragster will be doing over 250mph. The drag machine will continue accelerating to reach 330mph (530kph) after travelling just 1,000ft (300m) from the starting line.

£1,036
Average motor insurance premium for a UK driver in their 20s

£687
Average motor insurance premium for a UK driver in their 60s

Shaken, not stirred

Aston Martin is to release a real version of the famous James Bond DB5 fitted with outrageous gadgets including a revolving number plate. The limited run of 25 replicas of the iconic car from the 1964 film *Goldfinger* will each cost £2.75 million when delivered in 2020. The film car's legendary extras included: a powered bullet-proof shield that rose behind the rear window, machine guns that popped out from the front bumper, rear smoke deployment tubes and, best of all, a button to eject an unwelcome passenger through the sunroof.

The DB5 appeared in *Goldfinger*, alongside Sean Connery, then featured in a further six films: *Thunderball* (1965), again with Connery; *GoldenEye* (1995) and *Tomorrow Never Dies* (1997) with Pierce Brosnan and three appearances alongside Daniel Craig in *Casino Royale* (2006), *Skyfall* (2012) and *Spectre* (2015).

A measure of the car's impact was that the Corgi replica toy sold an astonishing 2.5 million models in 1965.

The revolving number plate and 'more functioning gadgets' will be included, says Aston Martin, but because of the on-board gadgetry, the silver birch DB5s will not be road legal in the UK.

In the last 100 years, most toy cars have been made from zamak, a little-known alloy made of zinc with small amounts of aluminium and copper added.

Road crossing 'lollipops' in some parts of the UK have been fitted with a heated handgrip. A special rechargeable strip embedded in the stick comes with a temperature dial, which can be adjusted depending on the weather.

---

14 songs about cars and driving

Cars – Gary Numan

Baby You Can Drive My Car – The Beatles

Drive – The Cars

Little Red Corvette – Prince

Driving Home for Christmas – Chris Rea

Mercedes Benz – Janis Joplin

Road to Hell – Chris Rea

Get Out of My Dreams, Get into My Car – Billy Ocean

Chitty Chitty Bang Bang – Dick Van Dyke

On the Road Again – Canned Heat

Radar Love – Golden Earring

Car Wash – Rose Royce

Little Deuce Coupe – The Beach Boys

Mustang Sally – Wilson Pickett

14 facts about the Model T Ford

The first models were dark blue, but when Henry Ford discovered that black dried quicker his slogan famously became you can buy them in "any colour you want as long as it's black".

By 1923, the Model T formed 52% of America's total car production.

Henry Ford studied Chicago meat-packing factories to devise his first automotive assembly line. By 1914, the Ford production line was so efficient it took only 93 minutes to assemble a Model T.

The starting handles used to fire up the Model Ts could be very dangerous. There are stories of them 'kicking back' and breaking an owner's thumb or an arm. Occasionally, the handle would be thrown off like a missile. Worse still, if the throttle lever on the steering column was not set properly the car would run you over as soon as it started.

Henry Ford didn't design the Model T. He left that his friend, engineer Childe Harold Willis, who also designed the Ford script logo that is still in use today.

Model Ts were also built at a factory in Trafford Park, Manchester. The car sold in the UK for £175.

Ford considered the Model T's main rival to be the horse or 'Dobbin'. In 1913 Ford advertised: "Old Dobbin weighs more than a Ford car. But he has only one-twentieth the strength, cannot go as fast nor as far, costs more to maintain and almost as much to acquire."

When only two roads existed in the entire US state of Kansas – one going north to south and one going east to west – two Model Ts crashed at the only intersection. Happily both drivers were unscathed.

As production got faster over the years the price of the car fell dramatically, from $900 to $440.

Because petrol was fed to the engine by gravity, and also because reverse gear had more power than forward gears, the Model T often had to be driven up a steep hill backwards.

Most Ts only had one door and one bench seat. The driver would usually slide across from the passenger side.

Henry Ford paid employees more than other car manufacturers but they had to sign a contract stating that as soon as they became financially able to do so, they had to buy a Ford.

A Model T's top speed was 45mph.

The T was so successful that, according to one survey, Ford was the seventh-richest man ever to live and the first-ever self-made billionaire businessman.

"The winner ain't the one with the fastest car, it's the one who refuses to lose."

Dale Earnhardt

One's cars

The Queen learned to drive in World War II and worked as an ambulance driver in the Women's Auxiliary Service. She is now believed to own cars worth around £10 million. They include:

 Daimler Phaeton – the first Royal car, dating from 1900.

 The State Fleet – customised chauffeured limousines for official engagements: three Rolls Royces, three Daimlers and two Bentleys.

 Land Rover Defender – a fleet of around 30 for the Royal household, and one special customised model for HM's personal use on her estates.

 Jaguar Daimler V8 Super LWB – for the Queen to drive herself on road trips.

 Custom Range Rover – long-bodied, with backward-opening doors and open-air top to wave to crowds.

 Aston Martin Volante DB6 – bought by the Queen for Prince Charles and since converted to run on bio-ethanol fuel.

The first use of the term 'sports car' to describe a motor vehicle designed for higher speed and more nimble handling is believed to have been in *The Times* in 1919. It wasn't until 1928 that the phrase was first used in the USA.

The UK's best-selling cars between 1970 and 1979 were:

1. Ford Cortina
2. Ford Escort
3. Morris Marina
4. Mini
5. Vauxhall Viva
6. Austin Allegro
7. Ford Capri
8. Austin 100/1300
9. Ford Granada
10. Hillman/Chrysler/Talbot Avenger

The original Cortina was due to be called the Caprino until Ford marketing bosses learned that it was Italian slang for goat dung.

Mary Ward, the 42-year-old Irish astronomer, author and artist, was killed when she fell under the wheels of an experimental steam car built by her cousins in 1869. She is thought to be the first person to have been killed by a motorised vehicle.

Top car-related video games for fun and influence

1. Outrun 1986
2. Mario Kart 1992
3. Ridge Racer 1993
4. Need for Speed 1994
5. Gran Turismo 1997
6. Colin McRae Rally 1998
7. Driver 1998
8. Burnout 2001
9. Forza Motorsport 2005
10. Grand Theft Auto Online 2014

There are 17 carriageway lanes side-by-side
on the M61 at Linnyshaw Moss, Worsley,
Greater Manchester – the most on any
stretch of British motorway.

Five things you might not know about Morgans

» The waiting time for drivers wishing to buy a new Morgan
from the Worcestershire manufacturer is currently around
six months. That's a comparatively rapid delivery, as it has
been as long as 10 years in the past.

» A Morgan is the only car ever to be displayed in the shop
window at Harrods. It was in 1911 and the car had
a price tag of £65.

» Early Morgans competed in motorsport events driven
by company founder Henry Morgan, a curate's son, with his
wife Ruth, a vicar's daughter, as his passenger.

» A 1960s Morgan Plus 8 could accelerate from 0–60mph
in just 5.6 seconds.

» Between 2008 and 2010 only 100 limited edition Morgan
AeroMax cars were built. Buyers included Richard Hammond,
Rowan Atkinson and Paul O'Grady.

In 1965, Ford introduced eight-track cassette audio systems that
it had helped invent as an optional extra. This convenient new
musical alternative to vinyl records quickly gained popularity.
Eight-track systems were soon being fitted to millions of new cars
and were even standard equipment in Rolls Royces and Bentleys.
By the 1970s, however, the compact cassette started to take
over the home audio market. By 1983, even Ford had stopped
offering the eight-track players.

"*There may be pleasure in being whirled around the country by your friends and relatives, or in a car driven by your chauffeur; but the real, the intense pleasure, the actual realisation of the pastime comes only when you drive your own car.*"

Dorothy Levitt

Pioneer Dorothy Levitt was Britain's first woman racing driver and taught Queen Alexandria to drive. Dorothy was dubbed 'The Champion Lady Motorist of the World' after completing the longest-ever drive by a woman in 1905: driving a De Dion-Bouton from London to Liverpool and back. She later wrote a handbook for women motorists that included the advice to carry a small hand mirror when driving in order to "hold the mirror aloft from time to time in order to see behind".

In 1903, Dorothy was summonsed to appear at Marlborough Street Assizes for speeding in London's Hyde Park. According to the police, she had driven at a "terrific pace" and, when stopped, said that she would like to drive over every policeman and wished she had run over the sergeant and killed him. The magistrate fined her £5.

In 2018, the most valuable car brands in the world (an economic assessment based on sales, reputation, global market, spread of activities and future prospects) were:

1.	Toyota	●●●●●●●●●●●●●●●●
2.	Mercedes	●●●●●●●●●●●●●●●
3.	BMW	●●●●●●●●●●●
4.	Ford	●●●●●●●●●●
5.	Honda	●●●●●●●●●
6.	Nissan	●●●●●●●●
7.	Audi	●●●●●●
8.	Tesla	●●●●●
9.	Maruti Suzuki	●●●●
10.	Volkswagen	●●●

12 facts about the Citroën Traction Avant

The Traction Avant was made using pioneering mass-production techniques. Buyers were so worried about these techniques that André Citroën devised the world's first crash test for the new model in 1932.

The Traction Avant has appeared in more than 1,300 film and TV shows, including a prominent role in *The Sound of Music*.

An early version, popular with Paris cabbies, was a nine-seater Familiale with an enormous 50ft turning circle.

In 1945, due to post-war shortages, the Traction Avant was sold without tyres. Customers had to supply their own.

Two major publicity events for the Traction Avant were driving a 5,000-mile tour of France and Belgium in just 77 hours and spelling out the name 'Citroën' right up the Eiffel Tower in lights.

André Citroën built a huge new factory to produce the Traction Avant and celebrated its completion by inviting 6,000 guests to a huge banquet inside.

A Traction Avant was pushed off the edge of a cliff by a team of men to show its integral strength. The car somersaulted several times before coming to rest. When the dust cleared the cabin appeared to be completely intact.

Traction Avants for the more affluent UK market were assembled in Slough, where they were given luxuries like leather trim and wooden dashboards.

The Traction Avant was the first to mass-produce three groundbreaking features still used in cars today: front-wheel drive, independent suspension on all four wheels and a unitary 'monocoque' construction without a separate frame.

In 1949, Pierre le Fou and his notorious band of jewel robbers called 'The Traction Avant Gang' hit the French headlines. He was public enemy number one and they were famous for constantly outrunning local police in their 81mph top-of-the-range 2.8-litre Citroëns.

The car was acclaimed by critics but within a year of its launch the company was bankrupt. Citroën himself became ill and died in 1935.

In 2002, a group of more than 30 Traction Avants owned by collectors drove from Los Angeles to New York without breaking down.

When 19th-century German watchmaker Karl Immisch moved to London, he started experimenting with electric motors. He was so successful that in 1888 he was paid to produce two pioneering electric cars for His Imperial Majesty the Sultan of Turkey Abdul Hamid II.

Prior to shipping, one of these was tested on London's streets by the workshop foreman but crashed into a horse-drawn carriage in Oxford Circus – "fortunately doing but little damage" it was reported at the time.

Despite plenty of media interest in the exported vehicles, Immisch didn't receive many orders and focused instead on producing a fleet of electric boats.

Celebrities who can't/couldn't drive

Albert Enstein	Justin Bieber
Arthur Smith	Kate Beckinsale
Barbara Streisand	Ken Livingstone
Charlie Watts	Marco Pierre White
Christina Aguilera	Noel Gallagher
David Bowie	Princess Margaret
David Mitchell	Ricky Gervais
Ed Sheeran	Robbie Williams
Elvis Costello	Russell Brand
Freddie Mercury	Sir David Attenborough

"You will never know the feeling of a driver when winning a race. The helmet hides feelings that cannot be understood."

Ayrton Senna

Car colours ranked for safety

1. Yellow	Stands out in all conditions – hence common taxi livery
2. White	Good contrast in dark but not as clear in fog and daytime rain
3. Orange	Statistically very safe but somewhat helped by its rarity
4. Gold	Good in most conditions except heavy rain amid other headlights
5. Cream	Strong contrast against road and darkness but can disappear in mist
6. Pink	Rare and stands out against roadside greenery
7. Silver	Considered sensible but hard to see in rain and mist
8. Green	Can be lost against rural backdrop
9. Red	Can be confusing in urban environments and hard to see in dark
10. Blue	Blends in during both day and night
11. Grey	Poor visibility in most conditions
12. Black	47% more likely to be involved in night crash than white/yellow car

35% of the
world's
population
drives on the
left-hand side
of the road.

Facts about the Monaco Grand Prix

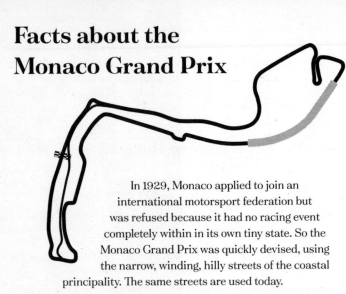

In 1929, Monaco applied to join an international motorsport federation but was refused because it had no racing event completely within in its own tiny state. So the Monaco Grand Prix was quickly devised, using the narrow, winding, hilly streets of the coastal principality. The same streets are used today.

The first race was won by William Grover-Williams in a Bugatti. Grover-Williams was half French, half British and during World War II became an undercover Special Operations chief in France, but was captured and executed by the Germans.

In 1931, the race was won by 55-year-old Louis Chiron, who was born and lived in Monaco. He remains the only resident to have won the Grand Prix.

Two drivers have crashed off the track and driven into the harbour. In 1955, race leader Alberto Ascari accidentally drove into the sea and had to swim to safety. In 1965, Australian Paul Hawkins span his Lotus, toppled off the edge of the harbour and was rescued by boat.

British driver Graham Hill won the race five times in the 1960s, earning the nickname 'The King of Monaco'.

Brazilian Ayrton Senna won the race a record six times.

McLaren is the most successful manufacturer with 15 wins.

American company Deeplocal has developed a luxury extra for car owners: a roof-mounted bottle cooler. The Blitzen device fixes to a car roof by magnets and can hold a bottle of any size, from a small beer bottle to a large champagne magnum, allowing it to chill thanks to the air passing over it.

TV appearances by the Triumph TR7

» A yellow TR7 was used by Purdey, played by Joanna Lumley, in *The New Avengers* (1976–7).

» Lucy Ewing, played by Charlene Tilton, in the 1980s TV series *Dallas*, drove a silver TR7 convertible.

» Lance Slater, played by Toby Jones, in the 2014 series *Detectorists*, drove a yellow TR7.

» In the 1976 TV film *Look What Happened to Rosemary's Baby*, Stephen McHattie plays the main character Adrian, who drives a green TR7.

The French-made De Dion-Bouton tricycle was Europe's most successful motor vehicle for several years at the start of the 20th century. The 211cc three-wheeler sold around 15,000 times and set a speed record of 67.8mph in 1902.

The dark grey Ford Mustang, driven by Steve McQueen in the dramatic movie car chase in *Bullitt* (1968), has long been one of the holy grails of high-end vehicle collectors. McQueen himself repeatedly tried to buy the distinctive 390 GT for the 11 years after the film was made until his death. The owners were unwilling to part with it at any price. The car has been immaculately restored by the American family that still own it and was borrowed by Ford in 2018 as part of the promotional events around the launch of a special 'Bullitt' Mustang edition.

The checked patterns on emergency vehicles are known as 'Battenburg markings' and have different colourways depending on the emergency service.
In the UK, there are:

Police Forces

Yellow/Blue

Ambulance and Doctors

Yellow/Green

Mountain Rescue

White/Orange

**Highways England
and DVSA**

Yellow/Black

HM Coastguard

Yellow/
Navy Blue

**Fire and
Rescue**

Yellow/Red

**NHS Blood and
Transplant,
Blood Bikes**

Yellow/Orange

**Rail
Response**

Orange/Blue

The fastest-ever production pickup trucks

(On a 0–60mph sprint, according to hotcars.com)

1. Toyota Tundra TRD Supercharged 2015 (4.4 sec)
2. GMC Syclone 1991 (4.6 sec)
3. Holden Maloo VXR 2012 (4.8 sec)
4. RAM SRT-10 2006 (4.9 sec)
5. El Camino 454 SS 1970 (5 sec)
6. Ford F150 Lightning 2003 (5.2 sec)
7. Ford F-150 Raptor 2017 (5.3 sec)
8. Ford F-150 3.5 Ecoboost 2015 (5.6 sec)
9. Chevrolet 1500 High Country 2015 (5.7 sec)
10. Ford F-150 Tremor 2014 (5.8 sec)

The Peel 50 is the smallest production car ever made. The single-seater weighs just 123lbs and includes a handle at the rear to simply lift it up to complete awkward manoeuvres.

According to DVSA figures for the second half of 2018, Upper Witton in Birmingham is the most difficult area in which to take your driving test, as 70.4% of tests end in failure. Inveraray offers the best chance of success, with only 15.1% failing their tests.

In England in 2016:

| 11% of household vehicles were parked in a garage overnight | 60% were parked on private property (but not garaged) | 25% were parked on the street | 3% were parked in other places |

Porsche power

In the Porsche Museum in Stuttgart visitors can see the first Porsche ever built. The 1898 C2 Pheaton was found in a barn in 2013 and restored. Visitors are usually surprised to discover that the first Porsche vehicle was powered by electricity.

Three firsts

1948 – Cadillac, Daimler and Lincoln all offer the first electric windows.

1951 – Chrysler presents the first power-assisted steering system to its customers.

1959 – The first record player built into a car's dashboard was offered by Chrysler, called the 'The Highway Hi-Fi'.

The first post-war Dodge Coronet models came with a unique three-speed automatic gearbox that was operated by a foot pedal. The Coronet continued in various generations from 1949 to 1976 and became the top-selling Dodge of all time with 2.5 million sales.

In the aftermath of World War II the German Volkswagen car plant and its machinery was offered for free to British motor manufacturers but none were interested.

The Panther Six was one of the most extraordinary British cars ever. The six-wheel, two-door convertible was produced in 1977. It was powered by a huge mid-mounted 8.2-litre Cadillac V8 engine with twin turbochargers. The four wheels at the front steered the car, two at the back powered it. It had a three-speed automatic gearbox, plus a built-in TV and telephone. Two were produced: one white, one black. Both still exist. Reports of a top speed over 200mph were unproven.

Tesla founder Elon Musk paid around £600,000 for the submarine Lotus Esprit that appeared in the James Bond film *The Spy Who Loved Me*.

"I couldn't find the sports car of my dreams, so I built it myself."

Ferdinand Porsche

Around 39% of cars on British roads are registered to a female driver, 61% to a male. The proportion of female owners has increased 6% in the last 20 years.

In 2018, *Autocar* magazine chose the 100 most beautiful cars ever. The top 10 are:

1. 1961 Jaguar E-Type Series 1 Coupé

2. 1970 Lamborghini Miura

3. 1959 Ferrari 250 GTO SWB

4. 1984 Ferrari 288 GTO

5. 1963 Porsche 911

6. 1935 Alfa Romeo 8C 2900

7. 1962 AC Cobra 289

8. 1962 Aston Martin DB4 GT Zagato

9. 2001 Aston Martin Vanquish

10. 1954 Mercedes 300SL Gullwing

Random car names

Nissan Cedric, SsangYong Chairman, Venturi Fetish, Suzuki Carry, Studebaker Dictator, Mitsubishi Pistachio, Renault LeCar, Ferrari LaFerrari, Great Wall Wingle, Mazda Scrum, Mitsubishi Lettuce, Mazda Bongo, Daihatsu Naked, Subaru Legacy Touring Bruce, Isuzu Mysterious Utility Wizard, Geely Rural Nanny, Volkswagen Thing, Peugeot Bipper, Suzuki Cappuccino, Renault Kangoo, Suzuki Esteem, Nissan Homy Super Long, Honda That's, Ford Probe, Mitsubishi Urban Sandal, AMC Gremlin, Nissan Fairlady, King Midget, Mazda Light Dump, Suzuki Joypop Turbo, Mazda Carol Me Lady, Bitter CD, Oldsmobile Futuramic, Chevrolet LUV, Isuzu Faster, Daihatsu Scat, Ford Flex, Hyundai Getz, Toyota Deliboy, Subaru Brat, Honda Life Dunk, Master Rocket, BMC Landcrab.

10 facts about the VW Beetle

The basic chassis and overall design of the 'people's car' was penned by Bela Barenyi, an 18-year-old Hungarian student in 1925. He didn't patent the design.

Austrian designer Franz Reimpiess designed the German WWII Tiger Tank, the enduring VW logo (for which he was paid 100 Marks) and the flat-four engine used in the VW Beetle.

In 1964 in Germany, VW offered $25 to any babies born in a Beetle. Within five years they'd paid out 125 times.

The last two Beetles ever built in Germany are preserved in wax at VW's UK Headquarters in Milton Keynes.

In 1972, the Beetle finally overtook the Model T-Ford as the best-selling car ever, with more than 15 million sales.

The Guinness World Record for the most people 'in' a VW Beetle is 57, but that was achieved by a team of climbers who filled the car and climbed all over it, utilising every area of body and roof.

Early Beetle imports in the UK were vandalised because of its association with the Third Reich.

The car was originally officially called 'Kraft durch Freude' or 'Strength through Joy'. That branding wasn't a great hit with buyers though and it was soon nicknamed the 'Volkswagen' or 'people's car'. In 1938, the *New York Times* likened it to a beetle and the name stuck.

The last original-style Beetle was produced in 2003, in Mexico.

In 1961, after eight months of running their new pizza company as a partnership, James Monaghan traded his half of the business to his brother in return for a used Beetle. The business grew, became multinational and is now known as Dominos.

Brands with the highest average annual mileage

1. Subaru 13,740 miles ------------------------

2. Ssangyong 12,136 miles ----------------------

3. Volvo 11,663 miles ----------------------

4. Nissan 11,090 miles ---------------------

5. VW 10,899 miles ----------------------

The top-selling motoring gadgets in the UK

according to Amazon (Jan 2019)

1. Car key signal blocker
2. Dehumidifier
3. Air freshener

4. Digital tyre inflator
5. Portable jump-start pack
6. DIY breathalyser kit

Buyers of the 2011 Mercedes CLS63 AMG – already a very rapid luxury coupé – were offered an optional 'Performance Pack' for an extra £6,500. Motoring experts pointed out that this expensive choice knocked just 0.1 second off the 0–62mph acceleration time and worked out at £200 per 1bhp increase in power.

The world's fastest lawn mower is a Viking that reached 134mph on a Norwegian runway in 2015.

Californian-based luxury vehicle builder Rezvani Motors has recently developed what it calls the ultimate off-road supercar. The Rezvani Tank X is based on a humble Jeep Wrangler with a tank-like heavy-duty body weighing more than four tons and powered by a massive 6.2-litre supercharged V8 'Hellcat' engine. The Tank X comes with powered doors and a thermal night-vision system. Prices start at £200,000.

"Somebody actually complimented me on my driving today. They left a little note on the windscreen, it said 'Parking Fine'."

Tommy Cooper

In extreme northern settlements like Churchill, Canada and Longyearbyen, Svalbard, it has become normal for residents to leave car doors unlocked in case someone is being chased by a polar bear and needs a safe place to escape.

Tragic solution

In 1967, Hollywood movie star Jayne Mansfield died after her car crashed under the trailer of a large truck. It highlighted the danger of the height difference between cars and lorries, whose trailer is usually at the height of the heads of passengers seated in a car. US safety officials acted to recommend the fitting of an 'under-ride guard' to prevent this sort of accident, a device which was known as a 'Mansfield bar'.

Adolf's car quest

While in jail in 1924, after trying and failing to seize power, Adolf Hitler wrote *Mein Kampf* and a letter to a Mercedes dealership asking for a car loan.

Hitler, who later owned a fleet of Mercedes cars, had his heart set on the 11/40 model, which at the time cost 18,000 Reichsmarks, much more than he could afford.

Hitler was released later that year and earned a sizeable sum from the royalties to *Mein Kampf* but it is not known whether he ever did any business with the dealership.

10 classic British car brands and who owns them

Vauxhall	Established in 1903, this Luton-based brand is now owned by the French PSA Group.
Rolls Royce	The classic luxury car maker is owned by Germany's BMW.
Mini	The iconic Mini brand is also part of the BMW group.
MG	The historic Morris Garages sports car brand is now part of Chinese company . SAIC.
Lotus	The famous sports and racing badge of Lotus has now been bought by Malaysian manufacturer Proton.
Land Rover	The world-famous maker of Land Rovers and Range Rovers is now part of India's Tata manufacturing group.
Jaguar	The traditional British sporting car manufacturer is also now owned by Tata.
Bentley	The By-Royal-Appointment luxury manufacturer is now a small part of the enormous Volkswagen Group.
Aston Martin	The maker of James Bond's favourite car has been taken over by a consortium of financiers from the USA and Kuwait.
Morgan	The Malvern-based maker of retro-styled roadsters dates back to 1910 and is still completely owned by the Morgan family.

Three pioneering sports cars

Jamais Contente
An electric engine, aerodynamic body and lightweight alloy wheels were the ingredients of the fastest car of the 19th century, which was clocked at 66mph (105kph) in 1899.

Ford 999
Bodywork on the Ford was dispensed with to save weight. Ford even reduced the suspension, steering and driver protection to a minimum in the 999. Ingenuity and focussing resources helped Henry Ford himself drive the 999 to break the World Land Speed Record in 1904. By reaching 91mph (147kph) the 999 became the fastest car in the world.

Blitzen-Benz 1909
The record-breaking German monster car used a huge 21.5-litre engine at the Brooklands Circuit in Surrey and was able to reach 141mph (227kph).

10 more celebrity car endorsements

Peter Crouch – **Hyundai Santa Fe**

Atomic Kitten – **MG ZR**

Atomic Kitten – **Seat Alhambra**

Atomic Kitten – **Toyota RAV4**

Delia Smith – **Proton Gen-2**

Fabio Capello – **Vauxhall Insignia**

Gok Wan – **Vauxhall Ampera**

Take That – **VW Caravelle**

Pixie Lott – **Citroën DS3**

Kylie Minogue – **Ford Ka**

The word 'taxi' is a shortened version of 'taxicab', which arose in Edwardian London as a short form of 'taximeter cabriolet'. Taximeter derives from German for a scale of charges and cabriolet was originally a type of horse-drawn carriage.

The 33p car

A six-year-old boy tried to buy his dad a new car for his birthday by posting 33p through a Mazda showroom's letterbox. The story, reported by Ananova.com, came from a dealership in Essex, who found the mysterious coins on the door mat with a note saying: "I want to get my dad a car. He wants a car from you please. My mum has got a car so I want my dad to have one. When is my dad going to get it?" The garage owner said: "At first we couldn't understand it. But we guess the boy and his dad must walk past the showroom regularly and maybe his dad said he liked one of the models."

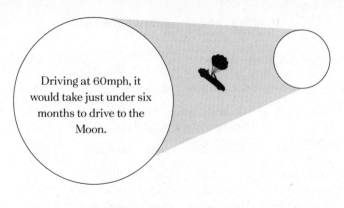

Driving at 60mph, it would take just under six months to drive to the Moon.

Seven facts about the Vauxhall Corsa

Corsa means race in Italian.

Early Corsas shared parts with the Lotus Elise.

Almost 10 million Corsas have been sold globally.

Celebrity Corsa owners include boxer Nicola Adams, musician Tinie Tempah, Artic Monkey Alex Turner and *Doctor Who* actor Matt Smith.

British police forces have bought 20,000 Corsas over the last 10 years.

After pensioner Peter Maddox's yellow Corsa was vandalised, Vauxhall renamed their yellow colour 'Maddox Yellow' in his honour.

The price of a Corsa has only risen by £3,850 in 25 years. Taking inflation into account the Corsa would be less expensive now than 1993.

The rise of the SUV

Small American manufacturer Crosley is believed to be the first to use the term sport utility vehicle to describe a convertible version of its station wagon in 1947.

Later, Ford used the term in 1966 to describe a two-door pickup version of the Ford Bronco and by 1974 Jeep marketed the first generation Cherokee as a sport utility vehicle.

The acronym SUV wasn't generally used until the 1980s. The term itself became fashionable in the 21st century and, by 2015, the SUV was the biggest-selling category of vehicles worldwide. By 2017, SUVs comprised more than a third of the global market for passenger cars.

Slowest new cars available in UK, with 0-62mph times:

1. Hyundai i800 MPV 2.5-litre 17.6 sec

2. Nissan Micra 1.0-litre 16.4 sec

3. Smart ForFour 15.9 sec

4. Citroën C1 semi-auto 15.7 sec

5. Fiat Doblo 15.4 sec

6. Peugeot 108 2-Tronic/Toyota Aygo x-shift 15.2 sec

7. Ford Fiesta 1.1 14.9 sec

8. Hyundai i10 1.0-litre 14.7 sec

9. Fiat Qubo 1.4 14.7 sec

10. Dacia Logan MCV 1.0-litre 14.7 sec

The M25 around London is the third-longest ring road in the world at 117 miles long. Germany's Berliner Ring is 122 miles long, but both are eclipsed by Beijing's outer-most ring road. Known as the Seventh ring road, it's an enormous 621 miles long.

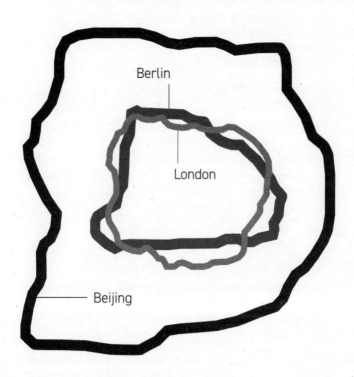

Berlin

London

Beijing

10 facts about
the Citroën 2CV

Pierre Jules Boulanger took charge of Citroën in 1935 and announced he wanted to create a car for lower income buyers. This would be "an umbrella with four wheels that can carry four people and 50kg of potatoes or a keg, at a maximum speed of 60kph (37mph), with a consumption of three litres per hundred kilometres (94mpg) and low maintenance costs."

The original car had a 0–40mph acceleration time of 42.4 seconds.

Early 2CVs used the same type of screw all over the car. The engine was held together with four screws. The body was held together by 16 identical bolts.

Boulanger was insistent that the German army didn't get their hands on his 2CV prototypes for military purposes. He had them all hidden – built into walls in buildings or covered in haylofts. When the Nazis tried to take Citroën's tooling, he sent the machinery off in random directions across Europe. Eventually the Citroën boss was officially labelled an 'enemy of the Reich'.

Early 2CVs were nicknamed 'Cyclops' because they only had one headlight. They only had one indicator too.

Thanks to its unique suspension, Citroën was able to boast that the 2CV could carry a basket of eggs across a ploughed field without breaking any of the shells.

Another design stipulation was that it had to be tall enough to take front seat passengers to church on Sunday wearing their hats.

In 1954, Citroën launched the 2CV Sahara: a pioneering four-wheel-drive car with two engines each driving one of the axles. Even when fully laden, the Sahara could climb a sand slope with a 45% gradient.

Today, the UK has a thriving 2CV racing scene, with a series of events in a single-make championship and an annual 24-hour endurance race.

In 1982, the 2CV became a Bond car during a scene in the film *For Your Eyes Only*.

11 bespoke options offered by Rolls Royce

Dashboard veneers made from a tree on your estate

Mother-of-pearl detailing throughout the cabin

Personal motif inlaid by marquetry into dashboard woods

Bespoke compass on dashboard

Hand-embroidered personal designs on upholstery

Gold-plated designs on door sills

Cabin ceiling decorated with personal designs using hundreds of fibre optic lights

Body finished with paint made with crushed diamonds

Teak door lining

Ostrich leather seats

Bespoke paint colour exactly matching a favourite flower petal from your gardens

---

Bubbly tradition

When American driver Dan Gurney won the 24 Hour Le Mans race in 1967, he was handed a bottle of champagne on the podium. As a gesture to journalists who said he'd never win, Gurney shook and then sprayed the champagne at them. It had never been done before but made such an impact that race winners have done it ever since.

In the 1960s, Chrysler built a fleet of 50 jet-powered cars and tested them for more than a million miles across America. The Chrysler Turbine worked well but was so expensive to build and had such heavy emission problems that the project was abandoned.

World records

Gatwick Airport meet-and-greet valet parker Brodie Branch set a Guinness World Record by parking 50 different cars in 22 minutes 16.7 seconds in an airport car park in 2012. The cars ranged from a Fiat 500 to a BMW 5 Series.

Mexicans Ernesta Hernandez Ambrosio and Jesús Juárez Vite spent more than three days setting a new Guinness World Record by kissing their car non-stop for 76 hours in 2013.

In 2017, a Porsche Cayenne S diesel towed a 516-seat, 285-ton Airbus A380 for 42 metres as part of a publicity stunt at Paris Charles de Gaulle Airport. Previously the record was held by a Nissan Patrol, which towed 170 tons of airplane in 2013.

In 2018, a Malaysian sultan was given a replica of the Flintstones car from the 1960s cartoon. Sultan Ibrahim Sultan Iskandar, ruler of the state of Johor, was given a working replica by a royal friend from a neighbouring state. Unlike the original, which caveman Fred Flintstone had to power with his feet, the sultan's car came with its own engine.

The most affordable cars to own*

1. Dacia Duster

2. Dacia Sandero

3. Dacia Logan

4. Suzuki Celerio

5. Mazda 2

6. Kia Picanto

7. Toyota Aygo

8. Peugeot 108

(*Cap hpi survey in 2018)

One in six jobs advertised in the UK require the applicant to be able to drive.

Rule 129 of the Highway Code states you must not cross a solid double white line in the middle of the road unless the road is clear and you are passing a stationary vehicle, bicycle, horse or road-maintenance vehicle travelling at less than 10mph. So, if it's a tractor doing 12mph, you would be breaking the law by overtaking.

The first car to use the initials GT was the Gran Turismo coupé version of the Lancia Aurelia in 1951.

Famous TV car ads

Nicole and Papa
Renault 1991 to 1998

Cogs
Honda 2003

Car being born
Audi 2015

Saab car racing a jet
Saab 1985

Changes
VW 1987

Transformers dancing car
Citroën 2005

Squeaky earring
VW 1990

Take my breath away
Peugeot 1988

Steve McQueen in Ford Puma
Ford 1997

Montego stunts on two wheels
British Leyland 1987

The force: youngster dressed as Darth Vader
VW 2011

Favourite things
Skoda 2007

Singing in the rain
VW 2005

The world's oldest endurance race

The 24 Hours of Le Mans is the world's oldest and best-known endurance motor race. It started in 1923 on public roads around the city in western France. In the decades of the annual race since, Porsche has won the most times, with 19 victories, including seven in a row from 1981 to 1987. The most successful driver is the Dane Tom Kristensen with nine wins, including six consecutive years.

Most Le Mans manufacturer wins

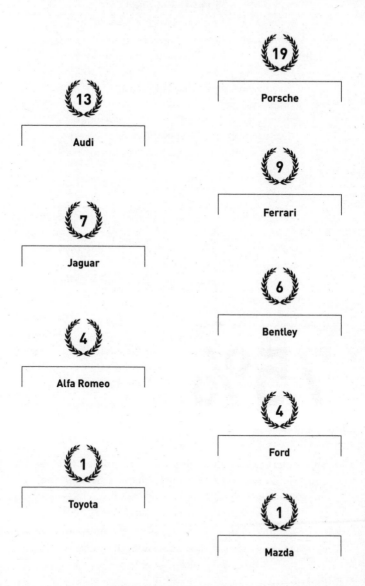

19 Porsche

13 Audi

9 Ferrari

7 Jaguar

6 Bentley

4 Alfa Romeo

4 Ford

1 Toyota

1 Mazda

Tail fins

American car designers competed to create the most
outrageous tail fins in the 1950s and 60s. The design trend
had started as an homage to World War II fighter planes
and became mixed with a little love for space age rocket-
powered science fiction. The result was cars like the 1959
Cadillac, built with the tallest fins of all: standing almost
four feet high and incorporating bullet-shaped
tail lights resembling a flying saucer's after-burners.

On 13 June 1895, French engineer and inventor Emile Levassor
drove his own homemade car with a four-horsepower Daimler
engine over the finish line in the world's first international
automobile race. Levassor completed the 732-mile course,
from Paris to Bordeaux and back, in just under 49 hours.
His average speed was a then-impressive 15mph.

75%

of the cars Rolls Royce
has ever built (since
1906) are still on the
road today.

At the end of March 2018 there were **37.9 million** vehicles
licensed for use on the UK's roads. Of these, **31.3 million**
were cars. The number of vehicles in the UK has increased
almost every year since World War II.

Currently statistics show that the number of vans is rising much
faster than the number of cars. Meanwhile, the number of heavy
good vehicles is falling.

Japanese scientists have created the world's smallest working car – a replica of Toyota's vintage Model AA. It's the size of a single grain of rice yet powered by a 600rpm engine. The tiny Toyota measures just 4.78mm long and is a 1/1000-scale version of Toyota's first passenger car. The miniature Model AA was built by technicians at the Japan Electric Company. It has front-wheel drive and is powered by a three-volt electric motor that has just five moving parts.

The Toyota Land Cruiser has been produced by the Japanese company without a break since 1951.

Truck mechanic Bob Chandler fitted huge wheels to a pickup truck and created 'Bigfoot'. The first monster pickup truck was an immediate hit with American audiences. At one venue, in 1983, a crowd of 68,000 gathered to watch Bob drive Bigfoot over ordinary cars, crushing them under 'foot'.

After inheriting a massive fortune, English teenager Louis Zborowski took up motorsport. In the 1920s, he employed engineers to build four different enormous racing cars in the stables of his mansion. The cars were powered by huge Mercedes aeroplane engines up to 23 litres in capacity and Louis raced them at Brooklands. He christened each of them Chitty Bang Bang, most likely after the war-time slang for British officers obtaining a 'chitty' or leave pass to visit brothels. Young motor-racing fan Ian Fleming watched Zborowski and later immortalised the cars in his book *Chitty Chitty Bang Bang*, which in turn became an iconic film. Tragically, Zborowski died at the age of 29, crashing a Mercedes into a tree during a road race.

The best car interiors of the 1980s

1. Mercedes E-Class

2. Porsche 928

3. Citroën BX

4. Fiat Panda

5. BMW 8 Series

(as selected by Haynes motor manuals)

The box-like Ford Model B of 1932 became one of the coolest American cars after it launched the craze for DIY hot-rodding. Engines were tuned and bodies modified to create a 'Deuce Coupé' with the deuce referring to the '2' of the 1932 model. In 1963 The Beach Boys immortalised this cult car in the classic hit 'Little Deuce Coupe' and later a bright yellow Deuce achieved automotive immortality as bad-boy teenager John Milner's street machine in the 1973 movie *American Graffiti*.

Oxfordshire gardener Kevin Nicks has built a wooden garden shed powered by the engine from an Audi RS4. It was timed at 105mph on Pendine Sands in 2018.

On the right track

London engineer Bramah Joseph Diplock patented the world's first four-wheel-drive system – for a steam-powered traction engine – in 1893. He also devised the first caterpillar track in 1910. In 1915, he demonstrated to Winston Churchill how his pioneering track system could be used effectively in trench warfare. This is believed to have led to the development of the first military tank.

The term 'zebra crossing' is generally believed to have been coined by young Labour MP James Callaghan in 1948 when viewing new black-and-white designs for road crossings at the Transport Research Laboratory. Callaghan became Prime Minister in 1976, while 'zebra crossings' went on to be used all over the world.

"Deciding what car you drive is a major life decision."

Nora Arellano

The average car in the UK will have four owners in its lifetime.

The Duryea brothers, James and Charles, from Illinois invented America's first petrol-powered car in 1894. In March 1896, they sold their first commercial automobile, the Duryea Motor Wagon. Two months later, New York City motorist Henry Wells hit a cyclist with his new Duryea. The rider suffered a broken leg, Wells spent a night in jail and the USA's first traffic accident was recorded.

A used-car dealer in America has built a chain of eight-storey car vending machines. Without any staff to pay, the company claim their prices are much cheaper. Customers find car details online, press a button to select their choice and the car is lowered to ground level for them to drive away. Carvana now operates 11 of the car vending machines.

Mille Miglia

The Mille Miglia (or Thousand Miles) was an open-road endurance race that took place in Italy 24 times between 1927 to 1957 (13 before the war, 11 from 1947). Like the older Targa Florio and later the Carrera Panamericana, the MM made Gran Turismo (Grand Touring) sports cars from the likes of Alfa Romeo, BMW, Ferrari, Maserati, Mercedes Benz and Porsche famous. In 1977, the MM was reinvented as the Mille Miglia Storico for cars manufactured no later than 1957.

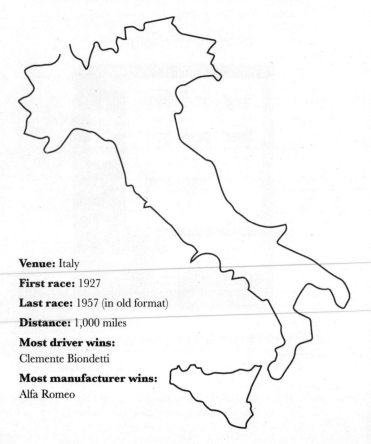

Venue: Italy

First race: 1927

Last race: 1957 (in old format)

Distance: 1,000 miles

Most driver wins:
Clemente Biondetti

Most manufacturer wins:
Alfa Romeo

Traditional racing colours

France	Blue (Bleu de France C79, M39, Y0, K9)
Germany	White/Silver
Italy	Red (Rossa corsa, C13, M100, Y100, K4)
Japan	White with red sun
UK	British racing green (C90, M44, Y92, K54)

Rocket propulsion

World War II hinted that the jet engine would revolutionise air travel. Perhaps, thought Rover Cars at the time, it would do the same for road vehicles too? It built a jet-powered prototype car that looked like an open-topped 50s roadster, but underneath the skin used the world's first road-going jet turbine. It featured on the cover of a popular science magazine with the headline: "Is this the future of motoring?" Jet 1 wasn't as unrealistic as it seems today. The jet turbine powered the wheels in the normal way and could run on a wide variety of fuels including petrol, paraffin or diesel.

But Rover discovered that Jet 1 was very unhappy at the low speeds most cars drive at most of the time. It was sluggish to start, but once warmed up its exhaust blew at scalding temperatures. Worst of all, fuel consumption was at best 6mpg. Rover persisted with turbine research and produced 142-mph turbine-powered sports cars that competed at Le Mans in the 1960s driven by later Formula 1 champions Jackie Stewart and Graham Hill.

Best-selling cars of all time

1. Toyota Corolla — 40 million sales
2. Ford F Series Pickup — 35 million sales
3. Volkswagen Golf — 27.5 million sales
4. Volkswagen Beetle — 23.5 million sales
5. Ford Escort — 20 million sales
6. Honda Civic — 18.5 million sales
7. Honda Accord — 17.5 million sales
8. Ford Model T — 16.5 million sales
9. Volkswagen Passat — 15.5 million sales
10. Chevrolet Impala — 14 million sales

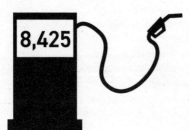

At the last count, there are 8,425 filling stations in the UK, dispensing more than 10 billion gallons of fuel a year.

Max Power magazine was a publishing phenomenon that revolutionised motoring journalism in the UK. The unruly, irreverent car magazine launched in 1993, reaching a circulation of around a quarter of a million a month before closing in 2011. *Max Power* was criticised for encouraging the 'boy-racer' trends that included modifications, but was a global success. Its annual live show attracted up to 50,000 visitors. Motoring personalities like Vicki Butler-Henderson and Jonny Smith began their careers with *Max Power*.

The moon buggy lunar research vehicles developed for the Apollo landings were designed with a top speed of 8mph. But Apollo 17 astronaut Eugene Cernan, who drove more than 22 miles around the moon's surface, managed to attain a speed of 11.2mph, giving him the first Lunar Land Speed Record.

Volvo invented the three-point seatbelt system in 1959 – then made the patent freely available to all other manufacturers in the interest of safety. Today, it is estimated that sealbelts save a life every six minutes.

Prince Albert of Monaco devised the first Monte Carlo Rally in 1909. It had the unusual feature of competitors starting from 11 different points all over Europe and converging on the principality. Racers were also judged on the 'elegance of their car and its arrival in Monte Carlo'. The inaugaural race was won by Frenchman Henri Rougier, who drove from Paris in a Turcat-Mery. A photo of Rougier and the car shows him in a suit and tie, wearing a panama hat and a carnation in his lapel.

Japanese invasion

The first Japanese car imported into America in 1957 was a single Toyota Toyopet Crown that had been originally designed as a taxi. By 1997, the Toyota Camry had become the best-selling car in the US. It retained that position for 19 years.

Stack of problems

An innovative automatic multi-storey car park opened in Woolwich, London, in 1961. The Auto Stacker used a totally automated system of conveyor belts and lifts to take cars to one of 256 spaces on its eight storeys. Sadly, the mechanisms were so complex they malfunctioned on the first day and within a few months the Auto Stacker was closed.

Motorsport enthusiast Dan Gurney and his team built their own racing car, the 'Eagle', for the 1966 Formula 1 season. The Eagle scored the only victory ever for an American-made car in F1 by winning the Belgian Grand Prix.

During a football match in October 2018 between Premier League Crystal Palace and non-league Dulwich Hamlet there was a repeated appeal over the stadium PA system for a car owner to move the parked vehicle blocking the emergency exit. Dulwich Hamlet goalkeeper Preston Edwards eventually realised it was his car. The goalie had to ask a member of the crowd behind the goal to move it for him.

A British driver's nose was broken by a frozen sausage that was thrown through the window of his car. An Essex ambulance spokesman said: "He was making his way home after work with the window down because it was such a nice afternoon. He saw a car coming the other way and felt a searing pain in his nose. Luckily he managed to stop his car without hitting anyone else."

A lot of lot

The world's largest car dealer is Longo Toyota in El Monte, California. It is spread over 50 acres and sells between 25,000 and 30,000 cars a year and as many as 5,000 in one month. The vast site includes a Subway, Starbucks, a Verizon phone store, two Enterprise Rent-a-Car locations and a AAA motor club office. There's also an on-site gym for more than 100 members of staff.

The grooves and patterns in the tread of car tyres are designed to deal with wet roads and remove water to maintain grip. Slightly worn tyres, with a bit less tread, actually have more grip than brand-new tyres on smooth dry roads.

Directional	**Symmetrical**	**Asymmetrical**
For wet traction even at high speeds	Even wear and long tread life	Ultra-high performance summer tyres

The residents of east Dorset own the highest proportion of cars in the UK: 694 per thousand people. The lowest proportion is in Hackney, London, with 170 cars per thousand.

The paper car tax disc was abolished in 2014. Since then they have become prized by collectors called velologists. Some discs have changed hands for hundreds of pounds and the values look set to rise.

Leading Italian tyre manufacturer Pirelli is the main sponsor of top Italian football team Inter Milan. It also sponsors Burton Albion's ground, who currently play in the English third tier. Their ground, The Pirelli Stadium, stands around the corner from Pirelli's UK factory.

Rubber tracks

In 1964, American Norman Craig Breedlove lost control of his jet-powered car on the Bonneville Salt Flats at an unknown speed, leaving skid marks nearly six miles long. The longest skid marks recorded on British public roads were nearly 980ft long and were left by a Jaguar involved in a crash on the M1 near Luton in June 1960. The car was estimated to have been travelling at over 100mph. The UK national 70mph limit wasn't introduced until 1966.

Colours of taxis around the world

Berlin: beige

Hong Kong: red

Mumbai: black and yellow

Kuala Lumpur: orange

London: black

Lisbon: beige or black/green

New York: yellow

São Paulo: white

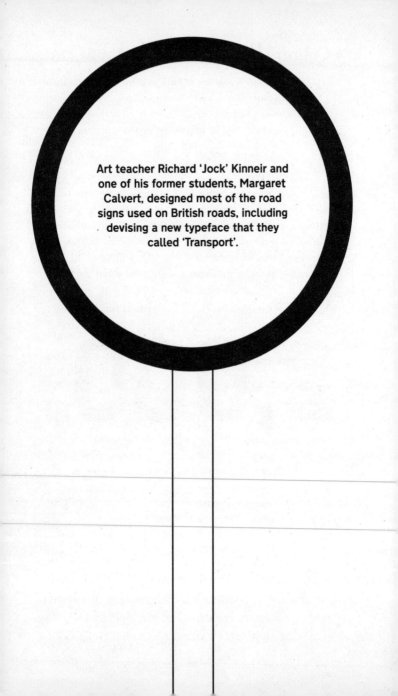

Art teacher Richard 'Jock' Kinneir and one of his former students, Margaret Calvert, designed most of the road signs used on British roads, including devising a new typeface that they called 'Transport'.

Ploughing ahead

The 1966 Jensen FF was the world's first high-performance car with four-wheel drive. The designers combined an American V8 engine, an Italian-styled body and the all-wheel-drive system from a Ferguson tractor.

A competition arranged by Swedish manufacturer Saab in 2011 judged the UK's best made-up family car games. The winning entry was called 'Face Snap'. The game required backseat passengers to decide on four facial expressions. The players cover their faces and face each other. They then reveal their expressions and if they're the same, they shout 'Snap!'.

2,000 miles

In the 1950s, normal family cars needed servicing every 2,000 miles. This usually involved garage mechanics greasing more than a dozen moving parts by smearing oil on with their hands, as lubricant technology was still in its infancy.

The first Cadillac Deville featured a telephone in the glovebox. The model, without the on-board phone, went on to become the top-selling Cadillac of all time with 3.9 million sales (1959–2005).

Grey is the new black

The latest figures show that grey is the most popular choice for car colour in the UK. Grey has taken over from black, with 59% of new British cars being black, white or grey.

Chinese billionaire and poetry-lover Li Shufu is founder, owner and chairman of Geely, a giant manufacturing group that now includes the brands Volvo, Lotus, Proton and British-based taxi-maker LEVC.

American engineer Craig Breedlove's cars were pioneers of jet power, which means the wheels merely roll along while the vehicle is propelled by jet force. Breedlove took the World Land Speed Record several times in the 1960s and in 1965 became the first man to drive at over 600mph. In the same year Breedlove's wife, Lee, used his car 'Spirit of America' to set the Women's Land Speed Record.

Land speed records

YEAR	SPEED (MPH)	DRIVER	CAR
1997	763.035	Andy Green (GB)	Thrust SSC (Jet)
1983	633.468	Richard Noble (GB)	Thrust 2 (Jet)
1965	600.601	Craig Breedlove (USA)	S of A Sonic 1 (Jet)
1964	526.277	Craig Breedlove (USA)	Spirit of America (Jet)
1947	394.196	John Cobb (GB)	Railton Mobil Special (ICE)
1935	301.129	Sir Malcolm Campbell (GB)	Blue Bird (ICE)
1927	203.793	Henry Segrave (GB)	Sunbeam (ICE)
1905	109.589	Victor Héméry (FR)	Darracq (ICE)
1902	76.086	William K Vanderbilt (USA)	Mors (ICE)
1902	75.065	Leon Serpollet (FR)	Serpollet (Steam)
1898	39.245	Gaston Chasseloup-Laubat (FR)	Jeantaud (Electric)

courtesy of www.landspeedrecord.org (a History in Numbers website)

Tycoon Elon Musk launched one of his Tesla cars into space in 2018 by mounting it on a rocket. The red sports car was 'driven' by a mannequin in a space suit and the car stereo was set to play a David Bowie playlist on a loop.

The top-selling Lexus of all time is not a luxury saloon but an SUV, the Lexus RX (1998–present) with 2.75 million sales.

Air block

When American manufacturers started using aeronautical wind tunnel testing for the first time in the early 1930s, they found that their contemporary box-like cars were so bad at slipping through the air that they were more aerodynamic travelling backwards than forwards.

Council carpenter Carlos Sierra from Weston-Super-Mare told *Top Gear* magazine that he loved his Ford Sierra estate, despite the constant jokes. "It was worse when I had a Cortina and everyone kept saying 'you ought to get a Sierra', " he said. "A policeman came last week to investigate an attempted theft of petrol from the car and he was called PC Ford. We had a good laugh when I told him what my name was."

The Head of Component and Environmental Testing at the Motor Industry Research Association (MIRA), Eamonn Martin, was also a world-famous marathon runner. Martin won both the London and Chicago marathons, as well as a gold medal for the 10,000m at the 1990 Commonwealth Games.

28 car brands
not currently in operation

AMC	Mercury	Saturn
Austin	Morris	Singer
Daewoo	Oldsmobile	Sunbeam
Daimler	Packard	Talbot
Delorean	Plymouth	Tatra
Geo	Pontiac	Triumph
Hillman	Reliant	TVR
Hummer	Riley	Wolseley
Jenson	Rover	
Maybach	Saab	

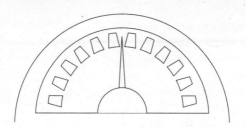

In 1958, the UK's first parking meter started operating in central London. The price of an hour's parking was sixpence (2½p).

Despite being born deaf, Hollywood stunt driver Kitty O'Neil held 22 different speed records when she retired in 1982. These included a new World Land Speed Record for Women Drivers set in a three-wheeled hydrogen peroxide-powered rocket car at a speed of 513mph.

Former army captain turned Ford product manager Terry Beckett developed a new car that was so successful that he ended up head of Ford UK, knighted, and Director-General of the Confederation of British Industry. The family car he developed, the Ford Cortina, was a monumental success thanks to his insistence on keeping it simple and reliable.

Suzuki's top-selling car of all time is the tiny Wagon-R (1993–present) with five million sales.

In an attempt to overcome the Ford's dominance in the US pickup truck market, GM engineers confessed they have joined public tours of its rival's Dearborn factory to see how the successful F-150 is made. The undercover engineers were trying to find ways to improve GM's Silverado truck, whose sales still lag behind the Ford by a wide margin.

A recent poll by *AutoExpress* magazine found the UK's most comfortable cars are:

1. Mazda CX-5

2. Lexus NX

3. Lexus RX

4. Kia Niro

5. Peugeot 3008

6. Land Rover Discovery Sport

7. Honda CR-V

8. Honda Civic

9. Toyota Verso

10. Vauxhall Mokka X

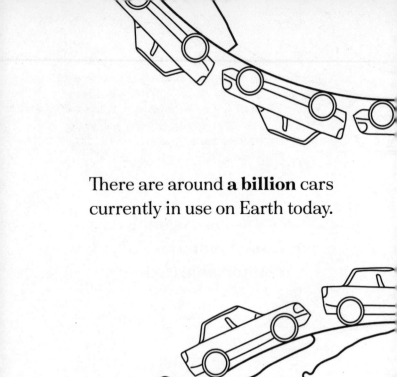

There are around **a billion** cars
currently in use on Earth today.

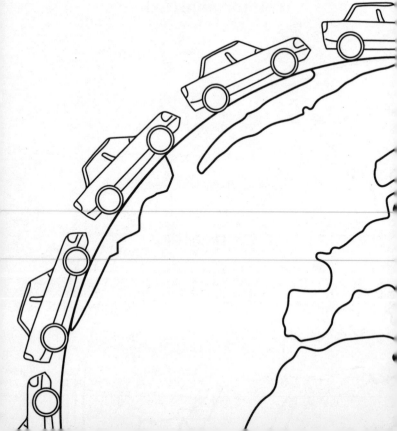

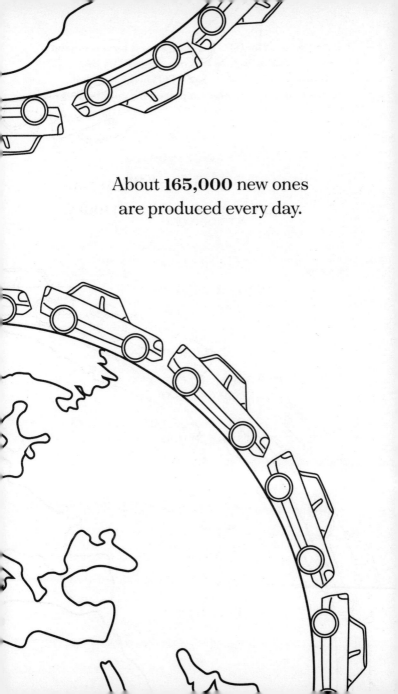

About **165,000** new ones
are produced every day.

A 1963 Ferrari 250 GTO was purchased for a reported $70 million in 2018 in a private sale, by the WeatherTech founder and CEO David MacNeil. It is reputed to be the highest price ever paid for a car.

Top 10 most expensive cars sold at auction:

1. 1962 Ferrari 250 GTO
$70,000,000

2. 1962 Ferrari 250 GTO
$48,405,000

3. 1962 Ferrari 250 GTO
$38,115,000

4. 1957 Ferrari 335 Sport Scaglietti
$35,700,000

5. 1954 Mercedes-Benz W196
$29,600,000

6. 1956 Ferrari 290 MM
$28,050,000

7. 1967 Ferrari 275 GTB/4 S NART Spider
$27,500,000

8. 1964 Ferrari 275 GTB/C Speciale by Scaglietti
$26,400,000

9. 1956 Aston Martin DBR1
$22,550,000

10. 1955 Jaguar D-Type
$21,780,000

Fan disaster

A German Michael Schumacher fan who tried to drive like his hero failed and demolished an entire street. The 28-year-old caused £200,000 of damage in Dusseldorf writing off his new £70,000 Ferrari and smashing into three parked cars, two bikes, a street lamp, a set of traffic lights, a billboard, a signal box and two trees, and left a number of houses without power. The driver emerged from the wreckage unhurt and told passers-by: "There was a problem with the gears."

The famous Alfa Romeo bonnet badge features the ancient arms of a Milanese family. This still shows a relic from medieval heraldry: a man-eating serpent. If you look closely at the badge you'll see a half-eaten human emerging from the mouth of the huge green monster snake.

"Keith Moon, God rest his soul, once drove his car through the glass doors of a hotel, driving all the way up to the reception desk, got out and asked for the key to his room."

Pete Townshend

Local Hertfordshire magician Alan Astra has owned a sequence of Vauxhall Astras. In recognition of this, the manufacturer have given him a tour of the Ellesmere Port factory. "My local garage know me and say 'here comes Mr Astra and his Astra'" he says. "I like it, it helps people remember me. And besides, the estate comes in handy for carting props around."

The best fast cars under £22,000

1. Ford Fiesta ST

2. VW Polo GTI

3. Peugeot 208 GTI

4. Mini Cooper S

5. Renault Clio RS

6. Alfa Romeo Mito Veloce

7. Vauxhall Corsa VXR

8. Seat Ibiza FR 1.5 TSI Evo

9. Suzuki Swift Sport

10. Abarth 595

When the Ford Cortina launched in 1962 the base model cost £639, undercutting its main rival, the £675 Morris 1100.

10 facts about the Jeep

After an urgent US government
request, the original mechanical
design for the Jeep was done in
just two days.

The name Jeep is probably derived
from a military acronym 'GP'
standing for General Purpose or
Government Purposes.

The US government initially ordered 1,500 Jeeps
from Willys and Ford in 1941, but the vehicle
became so useful and successful during the war
that by 1945, the companies had built 361,400 and
277,900 vehicles respectively.

The wartime Jeep had no key.
You started it by pushing a
button on the floor.

In 1954, the Jeep had been converted into a
civilian-style vehicle, the CJ5. The design
was so successful that it remained in
production for 29 years until 1983.

Jeeps were also converted to run on railways. The wheels were replaced with train wheels and it could then pull wagons totalling 10 tons by rail.

The Jeep had four-wheel drive, a three-speed gearbox and a top speed of 45mph.

President Dwight Eisenhower said that the three most important pieces of equipment in World War II were the Dakota Transport plane, a bulldozer and the Willys-Overland Military Model MB, since known worldwide as the Jeep.

The Willy's Jeep had a seven-slot radiator grill. The manufacturer Jeep has used that as part of its corporate identity ever since.

Jeeps have been built in India under licence by Mahindra since 1960. Since 2016, Mahindra Jeeps have faced competition, however, from imported vehicles made by Jeep itself.

Canadian-American Challenge Cup

The Canadian-American Challenge Cup,
or Can-Am series, ran from 1966 to 1987
and was the closest thing ever to an
anything-goes race.

Cars could have engines of any size and
configuration and any aerodynamic add-ons.

Many outrageous cars were entered,
such as the 240mph Porsche 917/30 that
won all of the 1973 season's races except
two (which were won by the slightly less
outrageous Porsche 917/10). It could do
0–62mph in 2.3 seconds.

Canadian-American Challenge Cup
Winners 1966 to 1987

Year	Driver	Car
1966	John Surtees (UK)	Lola T70-Chevrolet
1967	Bruce McLaren (NZ)	McLaren M6A-Chevrolet
1968	Denny Hulme (NZ)	McLaren M8A-Chevrolet
1969	Bruce McLaren (NZ)	McLaren M8B-Chevrolet
1970	Denny Hulme (NZ)	McLaren M8D-Chevrolet
1971	Peter Revson (US)	McLaren M8F-Chevrolet
1972	George Follmer (US)	Porsche 917/10
1973	Mark Donohue (US)	Porsche 917/30KL
1974	Jackie Oliver (UK)	Shadow DN4A-Chevrolet
1975–1976	No Series	
1977	Patrick Tambay (FR)	Lola T333CS-Chevrolet
1978	Alan Jones (AUS)	Lola T333CS-Chevrolet
1979	Jacky Ickx (Bel)	Lola T333CS-Chevrolet
1980	Patrick Tambay (FR)	Lola T530-Chevrolet
1981	Geoff Brabham (AUS)	Lola T530-Chevrolet / VDS 001-Chevrolet
1982	Al Unser Jr. (US)	Frissbee GR3-Chevrolet
1983	Jacques Villeneuve Sr. (Can)	Frissbee GR3-Chevrolet
1984	Michael Roe (RoI)	VDS 002-Chevrolet / VDS 004-Chevrolet
1985	Rick Miaskiewicz (US)	Frissbee GR3-Chevrolet
1986	Horst Kroll (Can)	Frissbee KR3-Chevrolet
1987	Bill Tempero (US)	March 85C-Chevrolet

According to motoring legend, the original boxy profile of the Land Rover was first drawn in the sand at a beach by the chief engineer. The company commemorated this event in 2018 by paying a snow artist to carve an 820ft outline of a Land Rover 9,000ft up a snowy mountain in the French Alps.

The 1949 Saab 92 was designed by redundant Swedish aircraft engineers and the final bodylines were penned by a science fiction illustrator.

A recent survey of road accident data by a British legal firm found which first names are most likely to be involved in a crash out of more than 25,000 incidents:

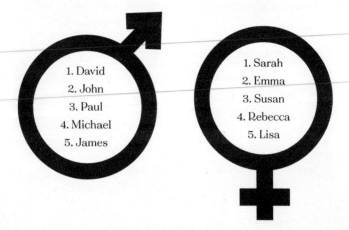

1. David
2. John
3. Paul
4. Michael
5. James

1. Sarah
2. Emma
3. Susan
4. Rebecca
5. Lisa

Artist Tracey Emin decorated four Fiat 500s with blue doodles in 2007 and they sold at auction for up to £200,000 each. Three years later, Damien Hirst covered an Audi A1 with paint splatters by rotating it on a 'paint wheel'. The colourful result sold for £350,000.

A Church of England bishop confessed to speeding in his car from the pulpit in front of the Queen. The Bishop of Blackburn caused giggles at Sandringham Church in front of Her Majesty when he told how he was caught by a speed camera and had to attend a speed awareness course in 2018.

Three intrepid motoring feats of the 1930s

Former army artillery officer George Eyston set a new world record for diesel-powered vehicles at Brooklands in 1934. He fitted the diesel engine from a London bus into a small Chrysler sports car and reached 115mph.

Colourful motoring journalist Dudley Noble entered the famous Monte Carlo rally in 1932 in a Hillman and towing a 14ft caravan. It was a promotional stunt for the pioneering new Eccles caravans. Noble finished 35th.

Swedish adventurer Eva Dickson became the first woman to cross the Sahara by car in 1932 after she made a bet with her lover Baron von Blixen-Finecke that she couldn't do it. Dickson continued her drive all the way from Nairobi in Kenya to her home in Stockholm. She won a crate of champagne from the Baron.

A man was arrested in York for driving an imaginary car. A street entertainer was apprehended by police in a shopping centre for pretending to be a Formula 1 car, wearing a red Ferrari uniform and holding a steering wheel. Police said it was feared he might cause an accident.

Every Aston Martin badge is handmade by jewellers in Birmingham's Jewellery Quarter using 21 stages of chroming, baking and polishing.

"He's not one of your smarter ones," said a police spokesman after a man in Louisiana, USA was arrested for trying to steal a police car containing a police detective and two US Marshals.

Inventive electrician Dave Arthurs of Springdale, Arkansas, spent $1,500 turning a standard Opel GT into a 75mpg hybrid in 1979 using a lawnmower engine, an electric motor and an array of six-volt batteries. *Mother Earth News* magazine published his story and 60,000 readers wrote in for the vehicle plans.

Lowest bridges on public roads in Britain

Auchendavie Road,
Kirkintilloch, Scotland

The Mill Walk, Northfield,
Birmingham, England

Bishton Road,
Bishton, Wales

Church Lane,
Govilon, Wales

Church Lane,
Neston, England

Ropewalk Terrace,
Neath, Wales

Top 12 countries building cars

USA
3.03 million
cars per year

UK
1.67 million
cars per year

France
1.75 million
cars per year

Spain
2.29 million
cars per year

Mexico
1.9 million
cars per year

Brazil
2.27 million
cars per year

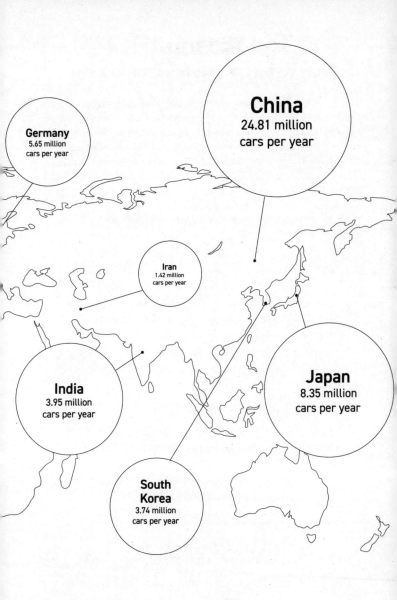

Germany
5.65 million
cars per year

China
24.81 million
cars per year

Iran
1.42 million
cars per year

India
3.95 million
cars per year

Japan
8.35 million
cars per year

South Korea
3.74 million
cars per year

How to buy a used Formula 1 car

The 50 F1 cars built each year eventually find their way to private dealers, like British specialists Memento Exclusives and Heritage F1. Run by former race team mechanics and drivers, these unusual car sellers are based in secret rural locations and offer millions of pounds worth of former F1 cars for sale, plus a huge range of souvenirs like gear parts and steering wheels. For example, a 200mph single-seater yellow Jordan EJ13 F1 car with its original Cosworth V10 engine driven by Giancarlo Fisichella and Ralph Firman in the 2003 season costs around £420,000. Cars without engines are cheaper; more successful cars are more expensive.

The Renault 4CV was developed secretly by French engineers during the Nazi occupation of World War II. The curvy rear-engined car was launched right after the war in a mood of national austerity: only one model was available and it only came in blue.

An American driver shot his car when it wouldn't start. The 64-year-old Florida man pulled out his gun and fired five rounds into the bonnet of his Chrysler. Neighbours called the police. When he was arrested the man said the car had "outlived its usefulness".

The first animated film featuring *Peanuts* characters Charlie Brown, Snoopy, Linus and Lucy was a US TV advert for Ford in 1959.

Japan and Finland have been judged to have the hardest driving tests in the world.

In 2017, an American car owner was woken at 5am by a car horn. Outside, he found a bear had broken into his Honda SUV looking for food but had accidentally locked itself inside. The bear trashed the car interior, then found the horn and kept pressing it until it was released and ran off.

Moustachioed former British naval officer Graham Hill became a world-beating racing driver. Hill was the only man to win the Motorsport Triple Crown: The Le Mans 24 Hour Race, the Indy 500 and the Monaco Grand Prix. He won the World F1 Championship twice and his son Damon went on to become World Champion too, the first father-son pairing to achieve the feat.

Number of cars left on UK roads*:

Ystava Yugo = 21

Rover Maestro = 197

Hummer = 275

Audi 80 = 1,563

Daihatsu Charade = 3,331

*according to howmanyleft.co.uk

*"If everything seems under control,
you're not going fast enough."*

Enzo Ferrari

Fastest production road cars*

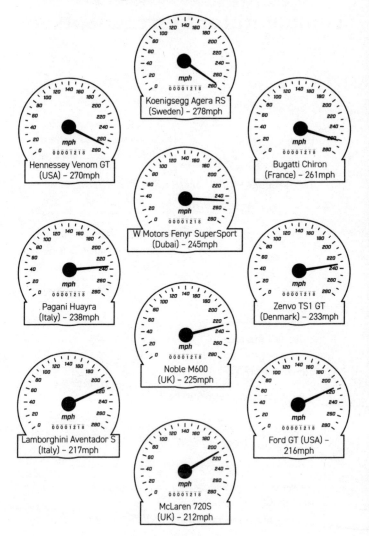

Koenigsegg Agera RS
(Sweden) – 278mph

Hennessey Venom GT
(USA) – 270mph

Bugatti Chiron
(France) – 261mph

W Motors Fenyr SuperSport
(Dubai) – 245mph

Pagani Huayra
(Italy) – 238mph

Zenvo TS1 GT
(Denmark) – 233mph

Noble M600
(UK) – 225mph

Lamborghini Aventador S
(Italy) – 217mph

Ford GT (USA) –
216mph

McLaren 720S
(UK) – 212mph

*At time of writing, ignoring concept cars, modified cars,
disputed or non-standard claims, according to *AutoExpress* magazine.

Quotes from motorsport commentator Murray Walker

"With half the race gone, there is half the race still to go."

"The lead car is absolutely unique, except for the one behind it... which is identical."

"This has been a great season for Nelson Piquet, as he is now known, and always has been."

"Even in five years time, he will still be four years younger than Damon Hill."

"You can cut the tension with a cricket stump."

"Andrea de Cesaris, the man who has won more Grands Prix than anybody else in the history of Grand Prix racing without actually winning one of them."

"Eight minutes past the hour here in Belgium – and presumably eight minutes past the hour everywhere in the world."

"He can't decide whether to leave his visor half open or half closed."

"I don't make mistakes. I make prophesies which immediately turn out to be wrong."

"This circuit is interesting because it has inclines and declines. Not just up, but down as well."

"Well, now we have exactly the same situation as at the beginning of the race, only exactly opposite."

"And now excuse me while I interrupt myself."

"There are seven winners of the Monaco Grand Prix on the starting line today, and four of them are Michael Schumacher."

Engineer's insight

Blind US engineer Ralph Teetor (1890–1982) invented cruise control. Teetor was inspired to invent cruise control one day while riding with his lawyer. The lawyer would slow down while talking and speed up while listening. This rocking motion so annoyed Teetor that he was determined to invent a speed control device. In 1945, after 10 years of tinkering, Teetor received his first patent on a speed control device which he called 'Autopilot'.

British sports car tuning specialists Lister claimed that its LFP was the fastest ever SUV when it was unveiled in September 2018. The vehicle is based on a Jaguar F-Pace and has been enhanced to offer a 200mph top speed.

The Fiat S76 was a record-breaking fast car with a tiny cockpit behind an enormous front bonnet section. It reached 137mph in 1911 thanks to its gargantuan 28-litre engine, the equivalent of about 30 small modern hatchback engines.

To promote a crackdown on illegal vehicle smuggling, Philippines authorities lined up 30 supercars and drove over them with a bulldozer. The crushed cars, including a Mclaren, Lexus and Audi, had been seized by customs in 2018.

Oxford garage manager
Cecil Kimber started selling
sportily modified Morris cars
in 1924. He quickly came up
with a simple badge for these,
using the initials MG inside
an octagon, which stood for
Morris Garages.

Dustin Hoffman's Alfa Romeo Spider in the 1967 film *The Graduate* was such a major part of the film that the manufacturer launched a special version for film fans, called 'The Graduate'.

Six things you might not know about the original Mini

Issigonis' original design was scribbled on a napkin in a Swiss restaurant.

Racing driver Stirling Moss was banned from driving for a year in 1961 for speeding in a Mini while testing it for a newspaper.

Minis in safari parks have been chased by lions that think they are prey.

In 1964, BMC built a prototype Mini with an engine at both ends. It was very fast but John Cooper crashed while testing it and the idea was dropped.

The world record is 66 people squeezed in one Mini.

In 1991, sales of Minis in Japan were higher than in UK.

In 1947, John Cobb's Railton Special used pioneering four-wheel drive, two boat engines and a fully-enclosed 'turtle' shell to become the first 400mph car. Few wheel-driven vehicles have since gone faster (jet-powered cars have taken over the land speed record instead). More than 70 years later the record for wheel-powered vehicles has only increased by 40mph.

You're nicked!

On 28 January 1896, the world's first speeding ticket was issued to motorist Walter Arnold. Arnold was a pioneering motor trader, selling imported Benz cars from Germany. He was spotted by a police constable as he hurtled through the quiet village of Paddock Wood in Kent. Arnold was driving at four times the national speed limit. It sounds worse than it was for his car was travelling at the humble speed of 8mph, when the speed limit was 2mph.

All cars were supposed to have someone walking in front of them with a red flag to warn pedestrians. Arnold did not. The policeman climbed on his bicycle and caught the car after a marathon five-mile chase. Arnold was sent before the local magistrate – and fined a shilling (5p in today's money).

Later that year, Parliament removed the requirement for a flag-bearer and increased the speed limit to 14mph. A race for motor enthusiasts from London to Brighton was organised to celebrate. It is still held annually. Fittingly, Walter Arnold took part in the first London-to-Brighton run, driving his own 'Arnold Benz' – it is not recorded what speeds he attained on the journey.

In 2018,
Lego built a promotional life-sized
Bugatti Chiron that you could actually
drive. The project took almost a year and
used more than a million pieces including
2,304 motors, 4,032 gearwheels and
2,016 cross axles. The finished
car weighs 1.5 tons and has a
top speed of 12mph.

America's love of drive-in movies reached a peak in 1958 when there were 5,000 of them across the country.

The prop car used as a flying Ford Anglia in the *Harry Potter* films was stolen from a British film studio in 2005. The body of the famous car, which in reality has no engine, was found by police six months later at the remote hilltop castle of Carn Brae in Cornwall with a tow rope attached to the bumper.

Five great cars from USSR/Russia

Marussia F2 (2010)
Luxury 340bhp SUV with powered sliding doors

ZiL 112 Sports (1960)
Two-seater with 6-litre V8

Lada Niva (1977)
Three-door utility SUV – became a worldwide success and is still being built

Marussia B2 (2010)
160mph mid-engined supercar

ZIS 101A (1939)
Sleek two-door 100mph convertible

An American vehicle builder called Boss Hoss Cycles offers a unique three-wheeler comprising a 6.2-litre V8-powered motorbike front end with the rear section of a 1957 Chevy car. The trike costs around £46,500.

Wolseley Motors was a luxury British car manufacturer founded in 1901 by Vickers, maker of armour plate, artillery and machine guns. By 1927, it was the UK's largest car producer.

A Japanese manufacturer unveiled a concept car that uses airbags all over the outside of the body. The dent-proof design of the Flesby II was a smash hit at the 2017 Tokyo Motorshow and it was promised for full production in the next decade.

Cars that are most likely to suffer from rust

(according to 2018 MOT records)

1. Ford Fiesta

2. Vauxhall Corsa

3. Range Rover Sport

4. Ford StreetKa

5. Toyota RAV4

6. Jeep Wrangler

7. VW Polo

8. Mini

10 facts about Brands Hatch

The first race on the Brands mud track was in 1926, for four miles, and didn't feature cars at all. It was an extraordinary race between cyclists and cross-country runners.

It originated as an oval on hilly fields belonging to Brands Farm. Dirt roads carved out by farmer Harry White's farm machinery were used by London-based pre-war cyclists to practice and run time trials.

In 1947, the track was grass and featured motorbike races. One was featured on BBC that year – the first bike race ever shown on TV.

Brands Hatch has been described as the best circuit in the world by racing driver Gerhard Berger.

In 1950, Brands Hatch opened as the UK's first purpose-built post-war racing circuit, after a £17,000 investment in tarmac to create the track. British motorsport legend Stirling Moss took part in the very first event.

During the London 2012 Olympics, the circuit played host to Paralympic events. Eleven years after losing his legs in a horrific race crash, former F1 driver Alex Zanardi won Paralympic gold at Brands Hatch riding a three-wheeled hand bike.

In 1986, a mechanical problem forced Nigel Mansell to race at Brands Hatch in his teammate Nelson Piquet's spare car, but he still won the last F1 race at the circuit.

The circuit is now owned by former F1 driver Jonathan Palmer (who made his F1 debut for Williams at the circuit in 1983).

Early races ran anti-clockwise but the racing line was reversed in 1954. This change resulted in the creation of the legendary Paddock Hill Bend, a fast sweeping downhill right-hander. An extension took competitors up to a right-hand hairpin, known as Druids Hill Bend.

Between 1964 and 1986, Brands Hatch hosted the British Grand Prix on even-numbered years. Jim Clark won the first race in 1964. In odd-numbered years the race took place at Silverstone.

"The way I drive, the way I handle a car, is an expression of my inner feelings."

Lewis Hamilton

Formula E racing driver Jean-Eric Vergne challenged the world's fastest mammal, a cheetah, to a race. Both were capable of 0–60mph in around three seconds so a promotional race was arranged in South Africa in 2018. The short race was very close but the car was first to the finish line by several millimetres.

The first hybrid vehicle, using both a petrol engine and electric motors, was built by self-taught young Austrian automotive pioneer Dr Ferdinand Porsche in 1898. The batteries were so huge the car weighed more than four tons.

UK racer John Surtees was the only man to win a world championship on both motorbikes and racing cars. Surtees was four times World Champion on 500cc bikes and Formula 1 champion in 1964 on four wheels.

The five steepest roads in the UK

Ffordd Pen llech, Snowdonia

Rosedale Chimney Bank, North Yorkshire

Hardknott Pass, Cumbria

Porlock Hill, Somerset

Bealach Na Ba, Scottish Highlands

40% gradient

33% gradient

30% gradient

25% gradient

20% gradient

A car's airbag inflates in just 30 milliseconds.

00 : 00 : 00 : 030

Scooby-Doo's Mystery Machine, a colourful cartoon minibus, is usually incorrectly identified as a VW Campervan. An investigation by the motoring website jalopnik.com concluded the fantasy vehicle was most closely related to a Chevy Sportsvan.

Musician and TV presenter Jools Holland owns an authentic looking Rover Jet 1 replica built from a Rover 80 and powered by a 150mph (241kph) Jaguar engine. Meanwhile, the original Jet 1 prototype is displayed in London's Science Museum.

Frog march

Lorry drivers who have been caught speeding are being made to hop like frogs. Police in parts of the Indian state of Bihar have decided to give humiliating punishments instead of taking offenders to court. One popular punishment involves making the drivers sit on their haunches, hold their ears and hop for almost half a mile.

The Gatso speed camera was invented by a Dutch rally driver Maurice Gatsonides in 1968, who used it to help him drive as fast as possible over practice courses. It was later taken up by police forces around the world.

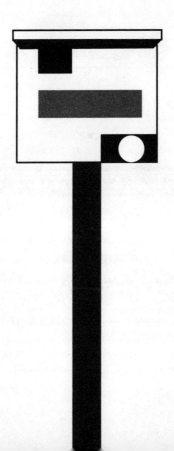

With its sweeping sporty lines, the Bugatti Type 57
Atlantic of 1936 is often chosen as the most
beautiful car of all time. Only four were ever built
and only two still exist. One is in the collection of
fashion designer Ralph Lauren; the other was sold
at auction in 2010 to a secret bidder.

The world's highest mileage car

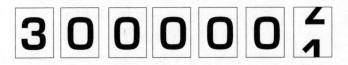

New Yorker Irving Gordon's Volvo P1800 has more than
3 million miles on the clock. He bought the coupé new in 1966
and has used it daily since. His advice to other motorists:
change the oil and filter every year or 10,000 miles.

Citroën has launched a pair of glasses that claim to be
able to cure car sickness. A pair of the €99 'Seetroen'
optics can be worn by anyone and can fit on top of
existing glasses. The tubular frames contain coloured
liquid which 'resolves conflict between the senses'.
The glasses were originally developed to combat
seasickness and have been 95% effective
in tests with French sailors.

In 1655, German watchmaker Stephan Farffler built the first
self-propelled carriage. Farffler was believed to have been an
amputee who designed himself a wooden three-wheel vehicle,
which was powered by handles that turned the front wheel.

The first mass-production car using modern disc
brakes was the Citroën DS in 1955. The DS used a
hydraulic system to power front disc brakes.
The following year, the Jensen 541 was the first
to feature disc brakes on all four wheels.

Top 10 nationalities of all drivers in the history of Formula 1

UK
🏎️🏎️🏎️🏎️🏎️🏎️🏎️🏎️🏎️🏎️🏎️🏎️🏎️🏎️🏎️🏎️🏎️🏎️ 173

Italy
🏎️🏎️🏎️🏎️🏎️🏎️🏎️🏎️🏎️🏎️🏎️🏎️🏎️🏎️🏎️🏎️🏎️ 108

France
🏎️🏎️🏎️🏎️🏎️🏎️🏎️🏎️🏎️🏎️ 77

Germany
🏎️🏎️🏎️🏎️🏎️🏎️🏎️🏎️🏎️ 62

USA
🏎️🏎️🏎️🏎️🏎️🏎️🏎️ 57

Brazil
🏎️🏎️🏎️🏎️🏎️🏎️ 32

Switzerland
🏎️🏎️🏎️🏎️🏎️ 27

Argentina
🏎️🏎️🏎️🏎️🏎️ 26

South Africa
🏎️🏎️🏎️🏎️ 24

Spain
🏎️🏎️🏎️ 22

Six cars designed to look older than they really are

VW Beetle Mk II (1997)

Nissan Figaro (1991)

Mini One (2000)

Chrysler PT Cruiser (2000)

Dodge Challenger (2008)

Fiat 500 (2007)

Six unlikely police cars around the world

Lamborghini Gallardo (Italy)

Bugatti Veyron (Dubai)

Dodge Charger (USA)

Volvo V60 Polestar (Australia)

Nissan Skyline (Japan)

John Deere Tractor (UK)

Toyota is one of the world's biggest motor manufacturers, but is still run by the same family that founded it four generations ago. In 1924, farmer's son Sakichi Toyoda invented an automatic loom and helped kick-start Japan's industrial revolution. His son, Kiichiro, started building cars as an offshoot of the company in 1933. In turn, Kiichiro's son Shoichiro became chairman and oversaw the creation of Lexus and the world's biggest-selling hybrid, the Prius. And Shoichiro's son Akio, a motorsports enthusiast, is now president of the global Toyota Motor Corporation.

Record breaker

Gloucestershire rally champion and stunt driver Alastair Moffat holds the following Guinness World Records for driving:

Tightest Parallel Park*

Narrowest Gap Driven through on Two Wheels

Narrowest Donut (rotating a car in a circular skid)

Fastest time for three cars to complete 10 Donuts

(*Alastair recently broke his own record by sliding a Fiat 500C into a space just 7.5cm longer than the car using a handbrake turn.)

The Mercedes 300SL of 1954 is widely considered the world's first supercar. It had gull-wing doors and a direct-injection engine that reached the speed of 160mph.

3,000lbs: the weight of the Mini balanced on top of a man's head for charity.

The Bentley Bentayga luxury SUV can be specified with a bespoke fly-fishing set. The fishing set is designed to fit neatly in the Bentley's boot and comprises four rods in leather tubes, comprehensive leather boxes of accessories and even a complete outfit of fishing clothes. Two catch nets are built into the sides of the boot, which has a waterproof floor. The fishing optional extra costs £80,000.

Intrepid off-roading

In 1954, three students from Oxford raced three from Cambridge in a driving equivalent of the Boat Race. The Trans-Africa Expedition was an unsupported trek in two Land Rover Series I vehicles to the foot of Africa and back. The 25,000-mile contest followed a bar-room bet between two students. The Land Rovers conquered deserts, mountains and jungles before the Oxford team finally won.

Stanford University has reported
that the average American eats
one in every five meals in a car.

Different names for four-wheel drive

With an all-wheel-drive system power is fed to all four wheels
of the car. It is also known as 4x4 or 4WD. Manufacturers'
marketing departments, meanwhile, have devised various
names for this system:

Alfa Romeo – Q4

Audi – quattro

BMW – xDrive

Ford & Lincoln – ControlTrac

Jeep – Quadra-Trac

Kia – KX

Mercedes – 4Matic

Mitsubishi – S-AWC

Mini – ALL4

Nissan – Attesa E-TS

Saab – XWD

Seat – 4Drive

Suzuki – Allgrip

Volkswagen – 4MOTION

Birthday treat

To celebrate the company's 70th anniversary in 2017,
Ferrari bosses announced a series of anniversary models.
Not the normal one or two special editions that any lesser
brand would offer, but an incredible 350 different ones.
Ferrari created 70 different liveries or colour schemes, each
referring to some famous car, event or owner from the past –
like the brown body of Steve McQueen's 1963 GTO, the
blue with a white stripe driven to victory by Stirling Moss
in 1961, or the red 'Schumacher'. Pre-launch demand was so
high that some buyers wanted to buy five in a certain livery.
Ferrari said they only allowed one per customer 'to be fair'.
All 350 sold before they were built.

The average ticket price to an F1 Grand Prix in 2018

China	$160	£121
Russia	$241	£182
Hungary	$261	£197
Bahrain	$261	£197
Canada	$295	£223
Australia	$311	£235
Azerbaijan	$323	£244
Germany	$348	£263
Italy	$361	£273
Spain	$361	£273
Britain	$412	£311
France	$412	£311
Japan	$414	£313
Austria	$421	£318
Brazil	$489	£370
Singapore	$501	£379
Belgium	$521	£394
USA	$560	£423
Mexico	$619	£468
Abu Dhabi	$632	£478
Monaco	$850	£642

A survey of garages in 2018 found that due to the increasing complexity of cars, it takes on average 23 minutes longer to repair a fault than three years ago.

Business tycoon and motorsport entrepreneur Bernie Ecclestone was once a keen rookie racing driver. He bought a Cooper F3 racing car and had some early successes in the 1950s. But he retired from the sport after a crash in which he was thrown from his car and landed alongside the track.

In the 1960s, US President Lyndon Johnson owned an amphibious car. The President would surprise guests at his ranch in Texas by shouting that his brakes had failed before plunging into a lake and casually sailing the car around.

More than 5 million drivers in the UK

are aged over 70.

"I don't sell cars, I sell engines.
The car I throw in for free since something
has to hold the engine in."

Enzo Ferrari